Modern Israeli
warriors guard their
ancient capital. This
picture was given to
me by my friend who
is one of the greatest
jet fighter pilots in
history. He captioned
it, "Hal, my friend,
don't worry about
Jerusalem. We will
take very good care
of her. Carry on!"

HAL LINDSEY
A Prophetical Walk
Through the Holy Land

HARVEST HOUSE PUBLISHERS
Eugene, Oregon 97402

I dedicate this book to my daughters,
Robin, Jenny, and Heidi Lindsey, who
have traveled through the Holy Land
and loved it since infancy.

A Prophetical Walk
Through the Holy Land

Hal Lindsey

Copyright © 1983 by Hal Lindsey
Published by Harvest House Publishers
Eugene, Oregon 97402

Library of Congress
Catalog Card Number 83-80121
ISBN 0-89081-381-7

Unless otherwise identified, Bible quotations in this
volume are from the New American Standard Bible,
copyright © The Lockman Foundation 1960, 1962,
1963, 1968, 1971, 1972, 1973, 1975, and are used
by permission.

Bible quotations identified *NIV* are from The Holy
Bible New International Version, copyright © 1978
New York International Bible Society, and are used
by permission.

Cover photo: World Wide Pictures.

Book design: Koechel/Peterson Design, Minneapolis, MN

Introduction

This has been a very exciting book to prepare. It is not meant to be a history of the Holy Land, although much critical history is included. Nor is it simply a manual for touring the area. Rather, I have sought to take the reader with me in much the same way that on many occasions I have taken friends on actual trips through the land of the Bible.

The sites with the greatest prophetic significance have been selected for special consideration. Some locations are significant because they are connected with the fulfillment of prophecies made hundreds of years before the historical occurrence. Others are important because they are the focal point of future prophetic events that are about to happen in this generation. In all cases I have sought not only to present the prophetical and historical significance, but also to apply the spiritual significance for our daily living.

May this book be a blessing and bring an understanding and love for the Holy Land.

Hal Lindsey

Contents

INTRODUCTION 5

Flowers Foreshadow
Messiah's Coming 13

ISRAEL, HISTORY'S
GREATEST WONDER 17

Miraculous Birth 18

Israel's History Foretold .. 19

Prophecy of the
First Dispersion 20

Prophecy of the
First Restoration 21

Prophecy of the
Second Dispersion 22

Masada 23

Prophecies of the
Second Restoration 27

EGYPT 28

Abraham's Prophecy Begins 32

THE RED SEA
MIRACLE 36

SINAI 39

JERICHO 47

JERUSALEM 52

THE TEMPLE 57

The Temple
Foundation Rediscovered . 61

The First Clue 64

The Second Clue 71

The Third Clue 73

The Fourth Clue 75

BETHLEHEM'S CHILD 78

Divine Providence
in Action 81

Shepherds Meet
the Great Shepherd 83

Jesus' Baptism at
the Jordan River 84

The Unique Baptism 84

Pool of Siloam 88

Pool of Siloam's
Greater Meaning 90

SEA OF GALILEE 92

MOUNT OF THE
BEATITUDES 97

CAPERNAUM 101

THE GARDEN
OF GETHSEMANE 106

THE INCREDIBLE
PROPHECY OF
BETRAYAL 110

THE JUDGMENT
OF JESUS 114

GOLGOTHA 117

THE GARDEN TOMB 125
Jesus Predicts
His Own Resurrection .. 128

TOWER OF
THE ASCENSION 132

THE UPPER ROOM 133

AKKO OR ACRE 143
A Lesson in Divine
Providence 144

QUMRAN 151

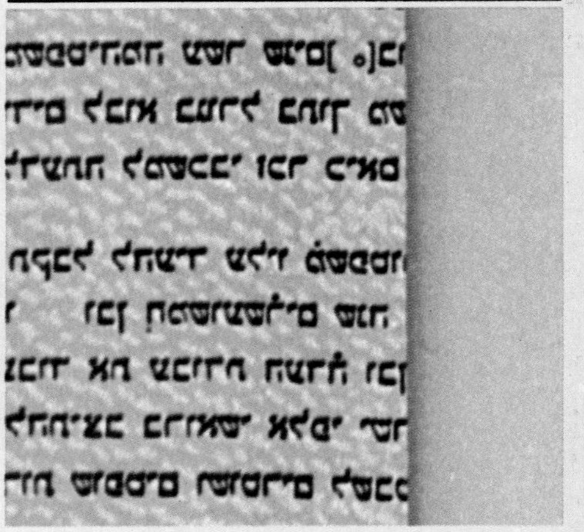

PETRA 161

Petra's Destiny 164

CAESAREA 169

PATMOS 174

Science Has Set
the Stage 178
Time to Look Up 179

MEGIDDO AND ARMAGEDDON 180

The Sequence of Battle,
Including Maps 185
Signs of
Armageddon's Approach . 198
A Sure Hope 198

A Prophetical Walk
Through the Holy Land

FLOWERS FORESHADOW MESSIAH'S COMING

The Judean hills east of Jerusalem toward the Dead Sea blossomed during the record rainy season of March 1983. A prophetic sign in themselves, these hills have not bloomed like this in all of modern history!

"The wilderness and the desert will be glad, and the Arabah will rejoice and blossom;

"Like the crocus it will blossom profusely and rejoice with rejoicing and shout of joy…

"For waters will break forth
in the wilderness
and streams in the Arabah.

"And the scorched land will become a pool, and the thirsty ground springs of water…."
(Isaiah 35:1,2,6,7)

"And you, son of man, prophesy
to the mountains of Israel and say,
'O mountains of Israel,
hear the word of the Lord.

"'O mountains of Israel,
you will put forth your branches
and bear your fruit for my people Israel;
for they will soon come.'"
(Ezekiel 36:1,8)

Streams of life-giving water flow in the normally arid and lifeless area of Wadi Kelt, in the Jordean wilderness near the Dead Sea.

Israel's climate and rain patterns are changing back to those of biblical times, returning the land to its ancient incredible richness. This shift is due in part to the tremendous number of trees that have been planted here. According to experts, this is helping to attract rain clouds. It is also fulfilling Ezekiel's prophecy.

These rare photographs show flowers growing profusely on top of Masada. They are almost symbolic of modern Israel growing out of a fallen kingdom and worldwide dispersion (*Ezekiel 37:1-14*).

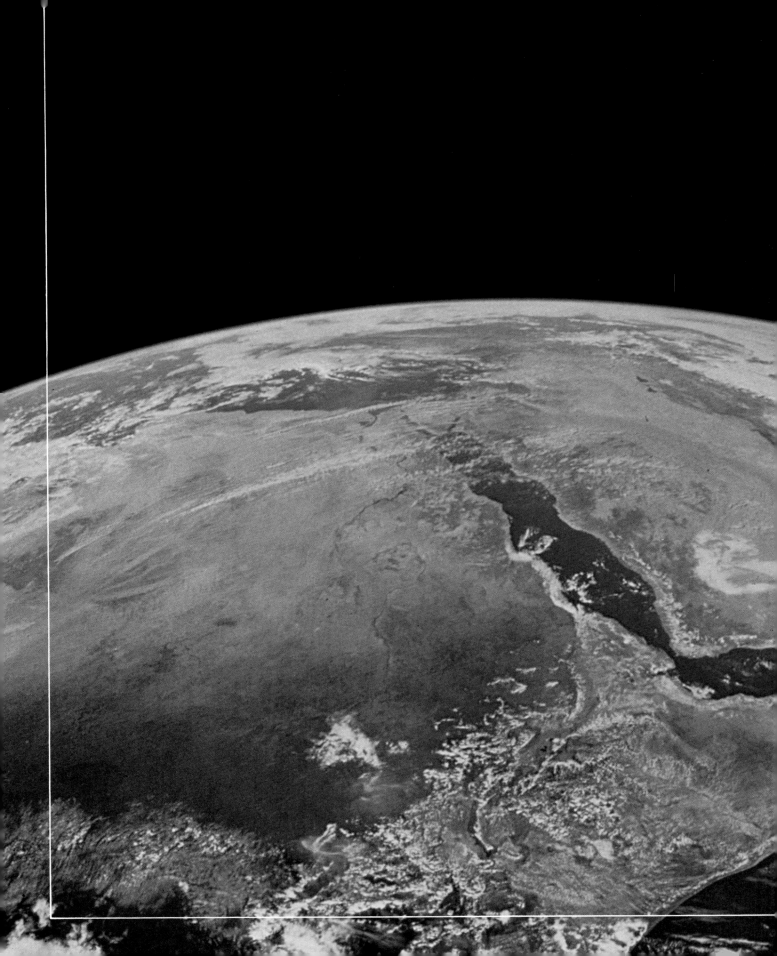

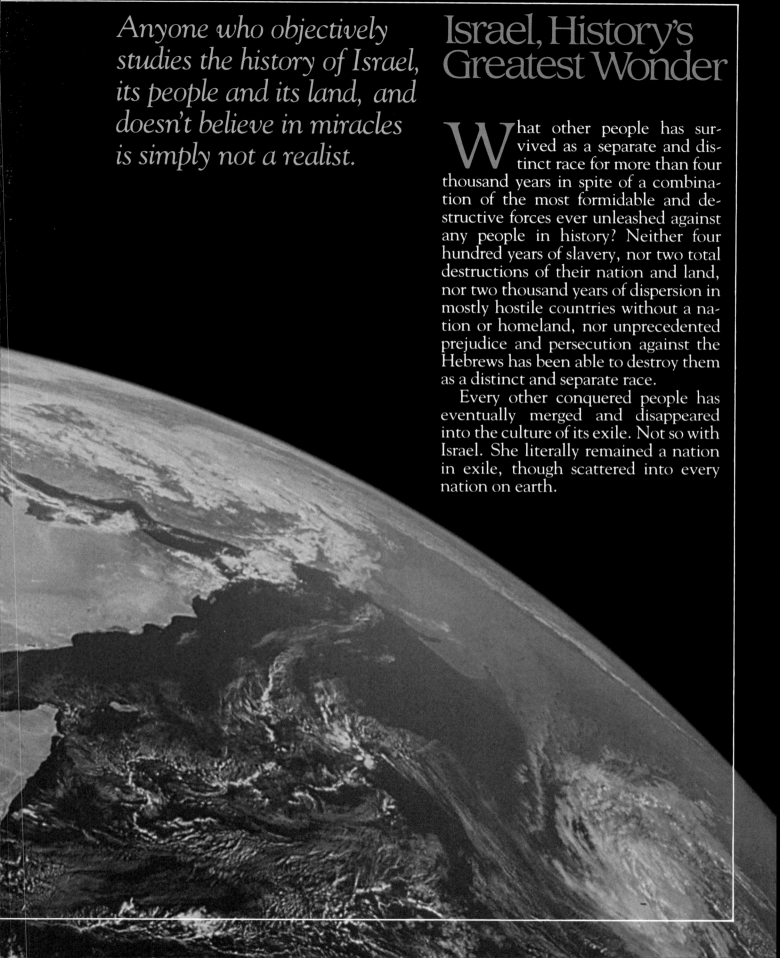

Anyone who objectively studies the history of Israel, its people and its land, and doesn't believe in miracles is simply not a realist.

Israel, History's Greatest Wonder

What other people has survived as a separate and distinct race for more than four thousand years in spite of a combination of the most formidable and destructive forces ever unleashed against any people in history? Neither four hundred years of slavery, nor two total destructions of their nation and land, nor two thousand years of dispersion in mostly hostile countries without a nation or homeland, nor unprecedented prejudice and persecution against the Hebrews has been able to destroy them as a distinct and separate race.

Every other conquered people has eventually merged and disappeared into the culture of its exile. Not so with Israel. She literally remained a nation in exile, though scattered into every nation on earth.

MIRACULOUS BIRTH

Israel's origin as a race began as a miracle. A rich Mesopotamian named Abram from ancient Ur of the Chaldees believed in the one true Creator-God in the midst of rampant idolatry. God called upon him to leave the comfort, wealth, prestige, and security of his home and go as a stranger to a dangerous and untamed land.

At a time when it was insanity to have possessions and live outside the security of a fortress city, God commanded Abram to dwell in tents. All of this required great faith on Abram's part and earned him a significant place in God's Hall of Fame recorded in Hebrews, chapter eleven (*Hebrews 11:8-19*).

Because of Abram's faith in God's promise to him concerning a son, God renamed him Abraham, which means "father of many nations." After many trials of faith, the promised son, whom God named Isaac ("laughter"), was born. Isaac's birth was a miracle because both Abraham (one hundred years old) and Sarah (eighty-six years old) were long past childbearing age. From Isaac's birth onward, the history of Abraham's descendants through Isaac and his son Jacob has been a pageant of triumphs and tragedies, ecstasies and agonies, punctuated by one miracle after another.

But through it all, whether willingly or unwillingly, the sons of Abraham, Isaac, and Jacob have been the vehicles through whom God has revealed Himself to the world.

A rich man, Abram (later Abraham) left the comfort and security of his home in Haran, heading out into the desert in obedience to God's call. His huge caravan included his wife Sarai, nephew Lot, all of their possessions, their servants, and their livestock. Because of his faith, God promised that he would be the father of a great nation.

ISRAEL'S HISTORY FORETOLD

The greatest wonder of all concerning Israel is that its history has been precisely foretold by a number of Hebrew prophets. Every significant event in the history of both the people and the land of Israel has been predicted with 100-percent accuracy. The following are but a few examples.

■ God revealed to Abraham that one of his descendants would be the source of blessing for all the nations (*Genesis 12:1-4*).

■ It was foretold to Abraham that his descendants would be slaves for four hundred years in a land not their own (*Genesis 15:13*).

■ Abraham was told that his descendants would be delivered in the fourth generation and that the nation that enslaved them would be judged (*Genesis 15:14-16*).

■ God told Abraham that He would lead the Israelites back to the land of Canaan and give it to them as an inheritance (*Genesis 15:16-21*).

Fulfillment:
The Messiah-Jesus' sacrificial death made forgiveness and salvation available to all nations (*Isaiah 49:5-6; John 3:16-18*).

Fulfillment:
The sons of Israel fled to Egypt to escape famine in Canaan and remained there for four hundred years.

Fulfillment:
Through Moses and the great devastating judgments upon Egypt, God delivered the people of Israel (*Exodus 1-15*).

Fulfillment:
Under Moses, the people were brought back to the Promised Land. Under Joshua, they conquered most of it. According to many later prophecies, the greater fulfillment will come when the Messiah returns in the last days to deliver Israel.

PROPHECY OF THE FIRST DISPERSION

■ Just before the Hebrews conquered the Promised Land, Moses predicted that Israel would twice be destroyed as a nation and twice be driven out of the land because of persistent unbelief. He also predicted that the first destruction and dispersion would come by the hand of one mighty nation. He specifically predicted that in this dispersion the Israelites would be taken captive into this ONE invading nation (*Deuteronomy 28:49-57*). **Fulfillment:** The Babylonians destroyed Jerusalem (586 B.C.) and took the survivors back to Babylon as slaves (*2 Chronicles 36:9-21*).

Jeremiah predicted that the Israelites (who in Babylon were first called *Jews*, meaning "from Judah") would be held captive for seventy years and then would be free to return to Israel (*Jeremiah 29:10-11*).

PROPHECY OF THE FIRST RESTORATION

■ Isaiah added another detail to this same prophetic event. Two hundred years before it happened, he predicted that a Persian king named Cyrus would be God's instrument to set the Jews free and enable them to rebuild Jerusalem (*Isaiah 44:28–45:6*). Now, just think of how incredible this prophecy is! It foresaw the conquering of Israel by Babylon; the conquering of mighty Babylon by Medo-Persia and the ascendancy of Persia over the Medes, which at first was the more powerful of the two nations. Most amazing of all, it predicted the name of the first Persian king two hundred years before he was born as well as the return of the first wave of Jewish exiles and the reconstruction of Jerusalem.

Fulfillment: The priests recorded the exact fulfillment of both Jeremiah and Isaiah's prophecy: "Now in the first year of Cyrus king of Persia—in order to fulfill the word of the Lord by the mouth of Jeremiah—the Lord stirred up the spirit of Cyrus king of Persia, so that he sent a proclamation throughout his kingdom, and also put it in writing, saying, 'Thus says Cyrus king of Persia, The Lord, The God of heaven, has given me all the kingdoms of the earth, and He has appointed me to build Him a house in Jerusalem, which is in Judah. Whosoever there is among you of all His people, may the Lord his God be with him, and let him go up'" (*2 Chronicles 36:22-23*).

PROPHECY OF THE SECOND DISPERSION

■ In the same message, Moses predicted the second destruction of the nation. He warned that the second dispersion would be much more extensive and severe than the first: "Then you will be left few in number, whereas you were as the stars of heaven for multitude, BECAUSE YOU DID NOT OBEY THE LORD YOUR GOD. And it will come about that as the Lord delighted over you to prosper you, and multiply you, so the Lord will delight over you to make you perish and destroy you; and you shall be torn from the land where you are entering to possess it. Moreover, the Lord will SCATTER YOU AMONG ALL PEOPLES, from one end of the earth to the other end of the earth...And among those nations you shall find no rest, and there shall be no resting place for the sole of your foot; but there the Lord will give you a trembling heart, failing of eyes, and despair of soul. So your life shall hang in doubt before you; and you shall be in dread night and day; and shall have no assurance of your life" (*Deuteronomy 28:62-66*).

Fulfillment: This part of Moses' prophecy was fulfilled in A.D. 70 when Titus and the Roman Tenth Legion crushed Jerusalem, destroyed the Temple and scattered the surviving Jews throughout the known world. So many were taken to the slave markets of Egypt that no one would buy them. This literally fulfilled Moses' dread prediction of Deuteronomy 28:67.

Jerusalem on fire—as it appeared in A.D. 70 when Titus and the Roman Tenth Legion sacked the city. (Model of Jerusalem.) Many Jews fled their homeland, taking their faith with them in a worldwide dispersion.

This imposing butte of Masada, rising above the wilderness of Judah, was impossible for the invaders to scale. To crush this Jewish rebellion, the Roman governor Flavius Silva used Jewish slaves to construct an earthen ramp to the top of the fortress.

When the Romans finally entered the Zealots' stronghold, they discovered that the nine hundred sixty men, women, and children had committed suicide rather than to be massacred or enslaved. This Roman "victory" ended the last vestige of Jewish resistance.

The Dead Sea viewed from the rampart of Masada. Note the walls of the Roman Tenth Legion's square encampment in the lower right of the photograph.

MASADA

A small remnant of Jews escaped the Roman holocaust of A.D. 70 and fled to Masada. Masada was an incredible fortress built by Herod on top of a large butte by the southwestern end of the Dead Sea. After a long and heroic stand against the Roman Tenth Legion, defeat became inevitable. The Romans, using Jewish slave labor, built an earthen ramp up to the walls of the fortress. The night before the Romans stormed the fortress, the nine hundred defenders—men, women, and children—elected to commit suicide rather than to be enslaved.

Masada has become a symbol of the fight-to-the-death spirit of the reborn state of Israel. All military officers are commissioned in a moving ceremony on top of Masada. They take a solemn oath that "Masada shall *never* fall again."

Four F15's fly over Masada. Israel's Air Force is considered by most military leaders to be the best in the world. Every Israeli officer makes this vow at the ancient fortress: "Masada shall never fall again!"

PROPHECIES OF THE SECOND RESTORATION

Moses, Isaiah, Ezekiel, Amos, Zechariah and many other prophets predicted Israel's second restoration as a nation in the "latter days." They predicted that the Jews would return to their ancient homeland after a long and terrible dispersion among the nations, and that they would miraculously become a nation again (*Ezekiel 36, 37*).

The most important factor in these prophecies is that God promises the Jews that once they have returned in the second restoration, their nation will never be destroyed again. However, the prophets do forecast that there will be a great war called "Armageddon" from which the Jews will be miraculously delivered. According to Ezekiel, this deliverance will bring great numbers of Israelites as well as Gentiles to faith in the true Messiah-Savior.

The dispute to trigger the war of Armageddon will arise between the Arabs and Israelis over the Temple Mount and Old Jerusalem (*Zechariah 12:2-3*). This photograph, taken from the Mount of Olives, shows the most-contested and strategic piece of real estate in the world. We are witnessing the escalation of that conflict today. Devout religious Jews are increasingly desiring to build a new Temple on the Temple Mount.

Jerusalem viewed from the southeast. Note the startling contrast between ancient and modern architecture. According to prophetic Scripture, the Messiah will one day enter Jerusalem through the Eastern Gate.

Egypt

Egypt has been an important factor in the history of God's dealings with His people Israel.

Throughout a good part of biblical history, Egypt was the cultural and intellectual center of the world. Egyptian genius inspired the Greek, Roman, and other Western civilizations that followed.

Egypt had already been a great, advanced civilization for more than a thousand years when Abraham fled there for refuge because of a severe famine in Canaan. As the patriarch approached Memphis, the Pharaoh's capital, he gazed upon the monumental Step Pyramid (pictured on facing page). This pyramid was already more

Egypt's ageless monuments reflect a remarkable civilization. At the height of their power the Pharaohs were demigods, intermediaries between the people of Egypt

Pharaoh Ramses II of Egyptian Dynasty XIX had this temple cut out of rock at Abu Simbel. When flooding caused by construction of the Aswan Dam threatened this famous monument, engineers carefully sliced it apart and reconstructed it piece by piece on higher ground.

and the gods. When Moses led the Hebrews out of Egypt to Canaan, Pharaoh was forced to recognize the infinitely greater power of Yahweh, their God.

One of the oldest kingdoms on record, Egypt goes back to 3100 B.C. In the time of the Hebrew patriarch Abraham, its capital was Memphis, the ruins of which are located near the Sphinx and pyramids shown here.

Guarded by the two-hundred-forty-foot lion with a human face, perhaps an image of Pharaoh Chephren, and the magical spells of Egyptian sorcerers, the gigantic pyramid tombs were plundered of their grave goods centuries ago.

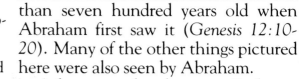

than seven hundred years old when Abraham first saw it (*Genesis 12:10-20*). Many of the other things pictured here were also seen by Abraham.

A few years after this visit, God gave Abraham a prophecy and promise concerning his descendants and Egypt: "And God said to Abram, 'Know for certain that your descendants will be strangers in a land that is not theirs, where they will be enslaved and oppressed four hundred years. But I will also judge the nation whom they will serve; and afterward they will come out with many possessions. And as for you, you shall go to your fathers in peace; you shall be buried at a good old age. Then in the fourth generation they shall return here, for the iniquity of the Amorites is not yet complete' " (*Genesis 15:13-16*).

This was a clear prophecy of the Israelites' long sojourn in Egypt. Abraham was given this prophecy long before his son Isaac was ever conceived.

A marvel of engineering, the "stairway to heaven" was a familiar sight to Moses and may have been seen by Jesus as a young Child. Now, thousands of years later, it remains one of the wonders of the world.

Photo on following page.

Photographed from the summit of the Great Pyramid, this splendid pyramid of Chephren at Giza still radiates the glory of ancient Egypt.

Yet it was fulfilled to the letter in a most remarkable way. In the third generation—after Isaac was born, followed by Jacob and his sons—an unusual situation occurred. Joseph was the youngest of Jacob's sons, and he was loved by Jacob more than all the others. Jacob climaxed his favoritism toward Joseph by making him a multicolored tunic. The older brothers were jealous because of this partiality. The final straw that incited them to put their hatred into action was a dream that God gave Joseph actually forecasting Joseph's reign over them (*Genesis 37:1-11*).

The brothers seized Joseph and sold him as a slave to an Arab caravan, which in turn sold him as a slave to the Egyptians. Through God's providence, Joseph became a ruler in Egypt second only to Pharaoh. During famine in Canaan, Jacob and his family fled to Egypt and wound up under Joseph's rule and protection. When Joseph's identity eventually became known to his brothers, they were terrified and expected fearful reprisals after the death of their father, Jacob. Joseph made a great statement of the divine viewpoint of life when he said, "Do not be afraid, for am I in God's place? And as for you, you meant evil against me, but God meant it for good in order to bring this present result, to preserve many people alive" (*Genesis 50:19-20*).

Joseph considered all the evil and trials brought upon him by his brothers' treachery to be God's providential way of saving the whole family. When we look at life's trials, we too should see that sometimes men plot them for evil but God means them for good. We should always claim the promise, "For we know that God causes all things to work together for good to those who love God, to those who are called according to His purpose" (*Romans 8:28*).

ABRAHAM'S PROPHECY BEGINS

Abraham's prophecy that "they would sojourn in a land not their own for four hundred years" began to be fulfilled with this providential move to Egypt. Joseph made a prophecy and promise to the children of Israel on his deathbed. He said, " 'I am about to die, but God will surely take care of you, and bring you up from this land to the land which He promised on oath to Abraham, to Isaac and to Jacob.' Then Joseph made the sons of Israel swear, saying, 'God will surely visit you, and you shall carry my bones up from here' " (*Genesis 50:24-25*).

For the next approximately three hundred fifty years, the primary reminder to the Israelites of God's promised deliverance was Joseph's unburied coffin. Whenever they saw the coffin, they thought of his prophecy and the oath concerning his bones. Joseph believed the prophecy of his great-grandfather Abraham, and this faith caused God to put Joseph in His Hall of Fame. "By faith Joseph, when he was dying, made mention of the exodus of the sons of Israel, and gave orders concerning his bones" (*Hebrews 11:22*).

As the time of the final fulfillment of Abraham's prophecy drew near, Moses was born. Through divinely arranged, extraordinary circumstances, he became the adopted son of Pharaoh's daughter. He grew up in the court of Pharaoh and was the heir-apparent to his throne.

Moses had the best education Egypt could offer, and he was a genius in the fields of mathematics, physics, engineering, and architecture. According to ancient reports, he built one of the Pharaoh's crown cities. He was also a military genius, having commanded

the Egyptian army in its defeat of the powerful Ethiopians. The Scriptures summarize this by saying, "Moses was educated in all the learning of the Egyptians, and he was a man of power in words and deeds" (*Acts 7:22*).

Moses' faith, when held up against the circumstances of his time, was awesome. There he was, a genius in many fields, the darling of Pharaoh and the Egyptian people, the heir-apparent to the throne of the most advanced, cultured, wealthy, and powerful nation on earth. Yet the Bible says, "By faith Moses, when he had grown up, refused to be called the son of Pharaoh's daughter; choosing rather to endure ill treatment with the people of God, than to enjoy the passing pleasures of sin; considering the reproach of the Messiah greater riches than the treasures of Egypt; for he was looking to the reward" (*Hebrews 11:24-26*).

As we look at these pictures, which bear testimony to the wealth and grandeur of the Egypt of Moses' era, we should be inspired to imitate his faith. Moses carefully weighed the privileges that his position in Egypt afforded him, every pleasure that the world could offer him. Having thought it through,

he considered the ultimate reward of being faithful to the Messiah and His call of greater value than all the treasures and pleasures of Egypt.

After Moses made the choice to follow God's will for his life, he had to be taught the paramount lesson of spiritual success—that God doesn't work on the basis of human strength or genius, but rather on the basis of divine power released by man's simple faith in His promises. It took God forty years to train Moses for the job of delivering Israel after he fled from Egypt, during which time he earned his B.D. (backside of the desert degree). Moses learned the hard way to be God-confident rather than self-confident.

At last the metal of the man was ready to be poured out of God's crucible. God sent Moses back to Egypt at the age of eighty, just in time to deliver the Israelites in exact fulfillment of the prophecy that He had given to Abraham. Through Moses, God unleashed devastating supernatural judgments against Egypt. The tenth judgment brought the mightiest nation of that day to its knees. Even the hardhearted and proud Pharaoh had to allow God's people to leave.

Ruins still reflect the rich artistic and architectural heritage of ancient Egypt. Ramses II, imaged in this statue at Luxor, was famous for his building projects. Moses, heir-apparent to the Egyptian throne, was the master architect and engineer of one of the Pharaoh's crown cities. According to Acts 7:22, Moses was *"educated in all the learning of the Egyptians, and he was a man of power in words and deeds."*

The Red Sea Miracle

God led the people out of Egypt by a pillar of a cloud by day and a pillar of fire by night. The Lord told Moses to camp in a shallow depression of earth between Pi-hahiroth and Baal-zephon with the Red Sea on the east. This, in effect, put the Israelites in a cul-de-sac. The Lord told Moses why: "For Pharaoh will say of the sons of Israel, 'They are wandering aimlessly in the land; the wilderness has SHUT THEM IN' " (*Exodus 14:3*).

God hardened Pharaoh's heart and he mobilized the mightiest army of that day. With hundreds of the most advanced chariots (comparable to main battle tanks today), he overtook Israel encamped in the cul-de-sac and immediately concluded what God had intended. Thinking that the Israelites were trapped, he ordered the horsemen and chariots to charge into the only opening of the cul-de-sac. From the human viewpoint, the Israelites were doomed to be slaughtered; they were a disorganized, untrained, and unarmed mob.

Bible teacher Bob Thieme taught me a lesson concerning this incident that has virtually saved my life many times. It may be summed up by the following two questions: Why did God deliberately lead these people into an apparently hopeless trap? and How did God expect them to react?

God led them into this situation because He wanted them to learn to believe His promises. Both Abraham and Joseph had predicted that God would deliver them from Egyptian bondage and then would give them the Promised Land of Canaan. Ninety percent of Abraham's prophecy was already fulfilled to the letter. The Israelites did go to live as strangers in a nation not their own; they were made slaves and oppressed for four hundred years; and God did judge the nation that oppressed them. So God expected them to believe that He would fulfill the final phase of the prophecy.

Even with his back to the sea, Moses reminded the panic-stricken Hebrews of God's promise of deliverance. Time and time again they had seen God prove His power and faithfulness as He brought supernatural judgments upon Egypt. Without the Hebrews' help, He had brought a mighty empire to its knees.

Photo on previous page.
The route of the Exodus viewed from space. The Red Sea miracle took place along the narrow tip of the Mediterranean Sea where it extends southward between Egypt and the Sinai Peninsula.

MOUNT PISGAH
(Mount Nebo)

KADESH-
BARNEA

MOUNT
SINAI

The arrows in the photograph show the approximate route of the Exodus from the Red Sea crossing to Mount Sinai. After a period of several months, God moved His people along the Gulf of Eilat to Kadesh-Barnea, where they failed to believe His promises. The Israelites then wandered in the wilderness for forty years. Afterward, they journeyed along the Wadi al Arabah, past the mountains of Edom and Moab to the Dead Sea. After command was passed from Moses to Joshua, the Israelites launched their conquest of Canaan, beginning at Jericho.

have seen My glory and My signs,

Now God expected the Israelites to look at the Egyptian army and the apparently absolute hopeless situation in the light of His promise. Even though they didn't know how God would deliver them, they were expected to believe He would take them to the land of milk and honey and give it to them, even as He had promised. They had all the evidence they needed to justify such a step of faith. The Israelites should have prayed something like this: "Lord, we don't know how You are going to deal with this mighty army, but since You promised to take us to Canaan and give it to us, and since You have worked mighty miracles to bring us this far, we can't wait to see what You are going to do with the Egyptians!"

We have a similar situation today. The Lord Jesus has already done the greatest thing possible for us who believe in Him. He has pardoned all our sins by dying for them in our place. He has delivered us from death and given us new life empowered by the Holy Spirit. He has removed every barrier that stood between God and us. So when He allows trials to come into our lives, He wants us to realize that HE allowed them in order to bless us and to teach us how to believe His promises.

Only one Israelite believed God that day —Moses. His faith in God's promises caused the Lord to open the Red Sea for His people and destroy the Egyptian army that tried to follow them.

The Suez Canal, at the point of the Red Sea crossing. Cornered in a cul-de-sac between Pi-hahiroth and Baal-zephon, with the Red Sea on the East, the Israelites faced extermination by Pharaoh's army. The Scripture says: *"Then Moses stretched out his hand over the sea, and all that night the Lord drove the sea back with a strong east wind and turned it into dry land. The waters were divided, and the Israelites went through the sea on dry ground, with a wall of water on their right and on their left" (Exodus 14:21 NIV).*
From the far side of the Red Sea, the Israelites looked back to watch the great Egyptian army following them into the sea—to destruction, for at God's command the sea went back to its place. At that point the awed Israelites *"feared the Lord and put their trust in him and in Moses his servant" (Exodus 14:31 NIV).*

This rocky path leads to the summit of Mount Sinai, the sacred mountain before which Israel camped on its wilderness journey. Here God revealed Himself to Moses and gave the Ten Commandments to the people through him.

Sinai

God led the Israelites into ten more *glorious opportunities to trust Him* as they went through the Sinai desert. Yet each time they failed to trust in God's promises. They failed to see that nothing is allowed into the believer's life apart from the Lord's will and purpose.

When the Israelites finally arrived at the Promised Land, they didn't even dare to enter it because of the report brought back by ten of the twelve spies sent in to scout the land. They cowered in fear when they heard of the warrior giants who lived there. The report of the other two spies, however, showed they had faith like Moses'. Their names were Caleb and Joshua. Caleb evaluated the situation, related it to God's promise, then stated the divine viewpoint perfectly:

"Then Caleb quieted the people [who were all panicked] before Moses, and said, 'We should by all means go up at once and take possession of it, for we shall surely overcome it…. If the Lord is pleased with us, then HE will bring us into this land, and give it to us—a land which flows with milk and honey. ONLY DO NOT REBEL AGAINST THE LORD [*i.e.*, by refusing to believe His promises]; and do not fear the people of the land, for they shall be our prey. Their protection has been removed from them, and THE LORD IS WITH US; do not fear them.' But the congregation said to stone them with stones" (*Numbers 13:30; 14:8-10*).

In reply to the congregation's unbelief, God said to Moses, "How long will this people spurn me? And how long will they not BELIEVE IN ME, despite all the signs which I have performed in their midst…. Surely all the men who have seen My glory and My signs, which I performed in Egypt and in the wilderness, yet have put Me to the test these ten times and have not listened to My voice, shall by no means see the land WHICH I SWORE TO THEIR FATHERS, nor shall any of those who spurned Me see it" (*Numbers 14:11,22, 23*).

Caleb and Joshua, who believed God's promises, were the only two who survived to go into the Promised Land. The rest died under the Lord's discipline as they wandered in the Sinai for forty years.

The Holy Spirit draws a tremendous lesson out of this bit of Israel's history, and it is the key to the whole Christian life for you and me today. I am going to amplify this scriptural quotation: " 'Today if you hear His voice, do not harden your hearts, as when they provoked Me.' For who provoked Him when they had heard? Indeed, did not all those who came out of Egypt led by Moses? And with whom was He angry for forty years? Was it not with those who sinned, whose bodies fell in the wilderness? And to whom did He swear that they should not enter His REST, but to those who were disobedient? [*Answer:* All except Caleb and Joshua].

"And so we see that they were not able to enter [God's rest] because of UNBELIEF. THEREFORE, let us fear lest, while a PROMISE remains of entering HIS REST, anyone of you should seem to have come short of it [*i.e.,* fail to claim and believe God's promises]. For indeed we have had the good news [of the faith-rest from worry and anxiety] preached to us, just as they also; but the word [PROMISES] they heard did not profit them, because it was not united by FAITH in those who heard. For we who have BELIEVED enter that REST, just as He has said..." (*Hebrews 3:15–4:3*).

The Israelites reached Mount Sinai three months after their departure from Egypt. Josephus, a Jewish historian, described Mount Sinai as "the highest of all the mountains that are in the country, and is not only very difficult to be ascended by man, on account of its vast altitude, but because of the sharpness of its precipices also; nay, indeed, it cannot be looked at without pain of the eyes: and besides this, it was terrible and inaccessible, on account of the rumor that passed about, that God dwelt there" (*Antiquities* II. xii. l; III. v. 1). Rugged and formidable, Mount Sinai represents the bondage of the Law (*Galatians 4:24ff.*).

Photo on following page.

Disciplined because of his disobedience, Moses was not allowed to enter Canaan. But God instructed him to climb Mount Pisgah and to look in all directions. From there God miraculously showed him the Promised Land as far north as Dan and west as the Mediterranean Sea.

Most people read the passage I've just quoted and miss the point because they think entering the Promised Land is a picture of entering eternal salvation. If that were the point, even Moses would not be saved, because for disciplinary reasons he didn't enter the land. Entering the Promised Land clearly illustrates the moment-by-moment REST that a believer enters when he stops going by his emotions, human experience, and human limitations and simply believes God's promises.

Canaan is a picture of supernatural victory through faith in God's specific promises. The Bible has more than seven thousand promises which deal with every possible need you and I will ever have in this life. God, through the writing of the Epistle to the Hebrews, challenges us to learn those promises and mix them with faith. Just as God led the Israelites into trials to teach them to believe Him, so He leads us today. The important thing is to recognize that nothing happens by accident in the life of a child of God. Whatever your circumstances, claim Romans 8:28 and then a specific promise that meets your need.

God showed Moses the Promised Land from this very mount, possibly on the very spot shown here. Moses was not allowed to enter Canaan because he became so angered by the unbelief of the Israelites that he failed to follow some very specific and important instructions. This sin occurred the second time that God made water stream from a rock in answer to the people's cry of thirst.

On the first occasion, God stood before Moses and the rock and told him to strike it once with his staff. When he did, water gushed out for all the people. But in order for Moses to strike the rock, he also had to strike the Lord, who was standing between him and the rock (*Exodus 17:6*). This is a divine "type"—a picture of salvation flowing from the Lord Jesus, who was smitten for sin in our place.

On the second occasion, Moses was commanded to simply speak to the rock and water would come forth. Moses, exasperated by Israel's continual unbelief, disregarded God's order. In fury he called the people "rebels," and he took God's glory for himself when he said, "Shall WE bring forth water for you?" Then he grossly disobeyed God by striking the rock twice instead of only speaking to it (*Numbers 20:7-11*).

The Lord had intended this act to be a type of the Holy Spirit flowing out to meet our needs in response to *believing prayer* to the resurrected Messiah. So as a result of Moses' disobedience, he was not allowed to lead the Israelites into the Promised Land. However, God graciously, supernaturally showed him the land from Mount Pisgah (shown on the preceding page).

St. Catherine's Monastery at Mount Sinai. Here Professor Tischendorf discovered the Codex Sinaiticus, one of the most valuable manuscripts of the whole Bible, being used by a monk to start a fire! The manuscript, first located here at Sinai, was taken to St. Petersburg, and then in 1934 it was purchased for the British nation. Scholars have dated it from the fourth century.

By a pillar of cloud by day and a pillar of fire by night, God led His people along the eastern side of Sinai and the Gulf of Eilat (or Gulf of 'Aqabah) of the Red Sea. They passed by ancient Elath on the northern end of the Gulf, a strategic port.

A crumbling Crusader fortress stands on an island in the Gulf of Eilat, along the route of the Exodus.

Archaeologist Kathleen Kenyon excavated this stone guard tower in the ancient Jericho ruins. It is estimated to be eight thousand years old. This makes it one of the oldest-known buildings on earth.

No doubt some soldiers of Jericho stood upon this very tower and watched the soldiers of Israel march around the walls of the city for seven days, performing their strange ritual of following priests blowing seven trumpets.

On the seventh day, the soldiers of Israel marched around the city seven times. At the end of the seventh trip, Joshua commanded the people to give a shout of faith, for the Lord had given them the city. As soon as they shouted, the walls of Jericho fell, the Israelites charged ahead and conquered the city.

The only people in Jericho who were spared were those related to Rahab. Her faith saved both herself and the entire family. God showed the greatness of His grace by taking this former prostitute and making her part of the direct family line of Jesus the Messiah.

Jericho

Joshua took command after Moses died. By the laying on of Moses' hands, he was commissioned and empowered by the Lord for the task of conquering the Promised Land. God gave Joshua several tremendous promises to claim in fulfilling his responsibility. I've meditated upon these promises many times and claimed them whenever God sent me out to do a difficult task. (*See Joshua 1:3-9.*)

General Joshua's battle plan for taking the land started with Jericho. This was a great fortress city which, according to modern archaeological research, was already several thousand years old in Joshua's day.

The photograph shows an ancient guard tower approximately six thousand years old. Looking up through the crevice made by archaeologists, you can see the Mount of Temptation, where our Lord Jesus did battle with the Devil at the beginning of His earthly ministry.

A great lesson of faith shines out of the conquest of Jericho. The Book of Numbers, chapters 13 and 14, records why the first generation of Israelites delivered from Egypt failed to enter the land of Canaan. They were afraid of the fortresses and especially the race of warrior giants called the Anakim. The following statement from the thirteenth chapter is a classic example of unbelief: "The land through which we have gone, in spying it out, is a land that devours its inhabitants; and all the people whom we saw in it are men of great size. There also we saw the Nephilim [the sons of Anak were part of the Nephilim]; and we became like grasshoppers IN OUR OWN SIGHT, AND SO WE WERE IN THEIR SIGHT" (*Numbers 13:32,33*).

The Mount of Temptation viewed from an excavation at Jericho. Mount Quarantania, traditionally the site where Satan tempted the Messiah for forty days (*Mark 1:12-13*), is seven miles northwest of Jericho.

When a believer fails to look at a trial in the light of God's promised ability to cope with it, he simply becomes paralyzed with unbelief and fear. The Israelites saw themselves as grasshoppers, so naturally they thought the Canaanites saw them that way too.

But here is the lesson. Forty-five years later, Rahab of Jericho revealed what was really going on in the minds of the Canaanites when the Israelites first spied out the land and made their report to Moses. She told two Israelite spies, "I know that the Lord has given you the land, and the terror of you has fallen on us and that ALL THE IN-HABITANTS OF THE LAND HAVE MELTED AWAY BEFORE YOU. FOR WE HAVE HEARD HOW THE LORD DRIED UP THE WATER OF THE RED SEA BEFORE YOU *WHEN* YOU CAME OUT OF EGYPT, and what you did to the two kings of the Amorites who were beyond the Jordan.... And WHEN we heard it, our hearts melted and no courage remained in any man any longer because of you; for the Lord your God, He is God in heaven above and on earth beneath" (*Joshua 2:9-11*).

The Scriptures reveal that God had already prepared the way for quick victory. The report of the Egyptian army's incredible destruction at the Red Sea had apparently spread throughout the civilized world during the year that the Lord led Israel to Canaan. Egypt was the mightiest power of that day, so such an incident would have been awesome international news.

The record of Israel's failure to believe God's promises and the awful consequence—wandering in the Sinai wilderness for forty years—serves as a warning to us today. But what a wonderful challenge and hope the incident can give us as well! God wants us to immediately commit all trials to Him and to believe His promises that apply to the situation.

Jerusalem

Jerusalem's importance is infinitely beyond its size and economic significance. From ages past, Jerusalem has been the most important city on this planet. Yet it never had the ingredients that have shaped and developed the world's major cities. It is not a seaport. It isn't on a great river. It was never on a main caravan or trade route.

Melchizedek came from this city to bless Abraham in 2000 B.C. (Jerusalem was then called *Salem; see Genesis 14:17-24*.) God directed Abraham to Jerusalem's Mount Moriah to offer his son Isaac as a sacrifice. When God spared Isaac by substituting a ram, Abraham called the place *Jehovah-Jireh*, which means "the place where the Lord will provide." God fulfilled that prophecy when He offered Jesus as a sacrifice for our sins on that very same mountain (*Genesis 22:14*).

David, the second king of Israel, conquered Jerusalem (then called *Jebus*) in about 996 B.C. He made it Israel's capital and placed the Ark of the Covenant there. From that time onward, Jerusalem became the spiritual center of the world.

More prophecies have been made concerning Jerusalem than any other place on earth, and every prophecy has been exactly and literally fulfilled. Near the end of the eighth century B.C., Isaiah predicted that the mammoth army of the Assyrian king Sennacherib would not destroy or conquer Jerusalem although it seemed certain the city would fall. God defended Jerusalem against him and the prophecy was fulfilled (*Isaiah 37:21-38*). Isaiah also predicted that the Babylonians would destroy Jerusalem and sack its Temple—one hundred fifty years before the city was taken (*Isaiah 39:1-8*).

Jerusalem! The mere mention of the name stirs emotions in people around the world.

A rabbi conducts a Bar Mitzvah ceremony at the hallowed Western Wall. Until the Six Day War when Israel annexed the Old City, this section of the Second Temple's retaining wall was called the Wailing Wall. Today it is simply called the Western Wall, a place of joy for God's chosen people. General Moshe Dayan declared on June 7, 1967, "We have returned to our holy places, never to part from them again."

Photo on previous page.

Sunrise over the Old City of Jerusalem. King David captured the Canaanite city in 1000 B.C. and made it his capital. When he established the Ark of the Covenant here, David centralized the faith of Israel's tribes. King Solomon built the First Temple here in the tenth century B.C. to enshrine the Ark and serve as a permanent house of worship. The First Temple was destroyed by the Babylonians.

After centuries of turmoil, Zerubbabel built the Second Temple and Roman-appointed King Herod later refurbished it. The Messiah predicted its fall, enraging His enemies. His prophecy was fulfilled to the letter when Emperor Vespasian's son Titus crushed Jerusalem. Not a stone of the Second Temple was left standing. Only a segment of the retaining wall remains. Prophetic Scriptures indicate that a Third Temple will be constructed here on Mount Moriah.

At an excavation near the Western Wall, archaeologists have uncovered beautiful, marble-columned streets dating back to the time of Jesus Christ.

While in Babylonian exile, the prophet Daniel predicted an exact timetable for the major events affecting Jerusalem. He predicted the edict that commenced the reconstruction of the city and its Temple. He said that exactly four hundred eighty-three years after the signing of the edict, Messiah the Prince would appear in Jerusalem. He said that the Messiah would later be rejected and killed. Daniel then predicted the destruction of the city and the Temple.

Once a week, shepherds trade at this sheep market by the wall of Jerusalem, as they have done for centuries.

The Old City's bazaars bustle with activity, linking modern Jerusalem with ancient cultures and traditions.

The Temple

Artaxerxes Longimanus of Persia gave the edict to rebuild Jerusalem and the Temple in 444 B.C. Exactly four hundred eighty-three biblical (three-hundred-sixty-day) years later, Jesus of Nazareth rode into Jerusalem on a donkey (*Zechariah 9:9*) and for the first time allowed Himself to be proclaimed Messiah and the heir to David's throne (*Luke 19:29-40*).

Jesus entered the Temple area by the Golden Gate, or the Eastern Gate, which lies precisely under the one shown in the photograph below. Jesus was rejected by the religious leaders. He then predicted the destruction of Jerusalem (*Luke 19:41-44*), saying it would occur in that generation (*Matthew 23:34-39*). Several days later, Jesus was crucified on Mount Moriah.

The Eastern Gate ("Gate of the Place of Sunrise") or Golden Gate was the main entrance to both Old and New Testament Jerusalem. The oldest and most famous gate of the city, it is the only one that led directly to the Temple. Jesus made His triumphal entry into Jerusalem through this gate, and He went through here on His way to pray in the Garden of Gethsemane.

Author Hal Lindsey with wife Kim and daughter Robin view a recent excavation of the Temple site showing the steps Jesus walked as He entered the Temple.

In A.D. 70, thirty-seven years after the above prophecy was given, Titus and his Roman legion destroyed Jerusalem and the Temple. This was an exact fulfillment of Daniel's prophecy (*Daniel 9:24-26*).

The final part of Daniel's prophetic timetable for Jerusalem and the Jewish people involves a seven-year period, commonly called the Tribulation. This will begin with the signing of a covenant between "the coming prince" of Rome and the leader of the Jewish people, called "the false prophet" (*Daniel 9:27*). This prophecy speaks of sacrifice and offerings which demand that the Jews rebuild the Temple for the third time upon its original site. At that point, Judaism and Islam will be placed on an inevitable course of war over the site, a war that will start Armageddon.

Many prophecies demand rebuilding of the ancient Temple, indicating that the event is a significant prophetic sign (*see Matthew 24:15 and 2 Thessalonians 2:3,4*). Therefore any move toward that direction is a crucial clue to what hour it is on God's prophetic timetable. For this reason I'm electrified with excitement by a recent development! For years most people have assumed that the ancient Jewish Temple's foundation was somewhere under the Dome of the Rock, but recent archaeological discoveries by Professor Asher Kaufman of Hebrew University have radically altered this conception.

The Dome of the Tablets and the Spirits, so-called because it is situated where the stone tablets of the Law were enshrined in the Temple, is one hundred meters away from the Dome of the Rock.

THE TEMPLE FOUNDATION REDISCOVERED

Dr. Asher Kaufman, a professor of physics at Hebrew University, has made the most exciting and important archaeological discovery of modern times. From the standpoint of biblical prophecy, it is one of the most crucial factors in a final alignment of predicted events that will precede the final seven years of history before the Messiah returns.

Dr. Kaufman, a crack archaeologist, spent sixteen years in intensive investigation on the Temple Mount before his findings were made known to the world in the March-April 1983 *Biblical Archaeology Review.* I am sure that it is not just coincidence that there have been three armed attempts by Jewish religious radicals to take over the Temple Mount since April 1983!

Although all of the extensive evidence upon which Dr. Kaufman bases his establishment of the Temple foundation's exact location cannot be given here, a few of the most outstanding facts are revealed in the accompanying charts.

The Eastern Gate of Jerusalem, shown at left, was sealed by the Moslems centuries ago. Their reason for closing this famous gate is unclear, but in doing so they unwittingly fulfilled the first part of the prophecy in Ezekiel 44:1-6 (*see 43:1-9*). The rest of the prophecy will be fulfilled when the Prince, Messiah Jesus, enters the Temple Mount through this gate, this time to rule.

THE FIRST CLUE

The most obvious clue that the Dome of the Rock *could not* be on the actual site of the ancient Jewish Temple is its position in relation to the important Eastern Gate. The many photographs of the Eastern Gate and the golden-domed mosque clearly show that the mosque is about one hundred meters south of a line drawn directly west from the Eastern Gate.

Ancient writings, including the *Mishnah,* indicate that the Eastern Gate led directly to the Temple, which faced eastward toward it. The photograph (page 65) of the model of Jerusalem in Jesus' day shows that the Eastern Gate was centered precisely on the east-west alignment of the Temple. The rare photograph (page 65) showing the top of the ancient Eastern Gate proves that the present gate was built exactly on top of the old one.

A line drawn from the center of the Eastern Gate, perpendicular to the city wall into which it was built, will pass right through the center of the Dome of the Tablets and the Spirits. This could not have been a mere coincidence; the Eastern Gate must have been purposely aligned with the place where the Ark of the Covenant rested within the holiest part of the Temple.

In one of the most remarkable discoveries of modern times, Dr. Asher Kaufman of Hebrew University has established that the First and Second Temples were built north of the Dome of the Rock. The Holy of Holies was actually situated under the little cupola called the Dome of the Tablets and the Spirits, which is aligned with the Eastern Gate.

This model is built to the scale and coordinates of the Second Temple of Jesus' day. Note that the Eastern Gate is in exact alignment with the center of the Temple.

Excavation beneath the twin-arched Eastern Gate (constructed by order of the wife of the Byzantine emperor Theodosius II in the fifth century A.D.) reveals the Temple Gate of Jesus' day exactly beneath the present gate.

In the photograph at the top of this page, you can see the area where the Third Temple will be constructed. Note the distance between the Dome of the Rock at left and the Dome of the Tablets and the Spirits at right. Underneath the Dome of the Tablets and the Spirits is the actual bedrock of Mount Moriah on which the Ark of the Covenant sat. The rest of the mosque platform is paved with flagstone, but this was left exposed.

When the Tenth Legion sacked Jerusalem in A.D. 70, the Temple was destroyed in exact fulfillment of prophecy. These stones of the Second Temple have remained just where they landed after being thrown from the wall by the soldiers.

Two select soldiers of the Israeli army are shown singing the Lamentations of Jeremiah on the anniversary of the destruction of both the First and Second Temples. Thirty thousand people gathered later that evening to lament the destruction of the old and pray for the rebuilding of the new.

Photo on following page.

"There is no God but Allah, and Mohammed is his Prophet." So states the Koran. Centered on the world's most violently contested tract of real estate is the third-holiest Moslem shrine, the Dome of the Rock. Jutting from the floor of this mosque on the summit of Mount Moriah is a rock sacred to the Moslems. Tradition maintains that Mohammed ascended into heaven from this site.

Evidence of the Temple's court wall has been uncovered.

This sloped rock mass is thought to be part of the Second Temple's foundation. It is in a garden north of the Temple platform and the Dome of the Tablets and the Spirits.

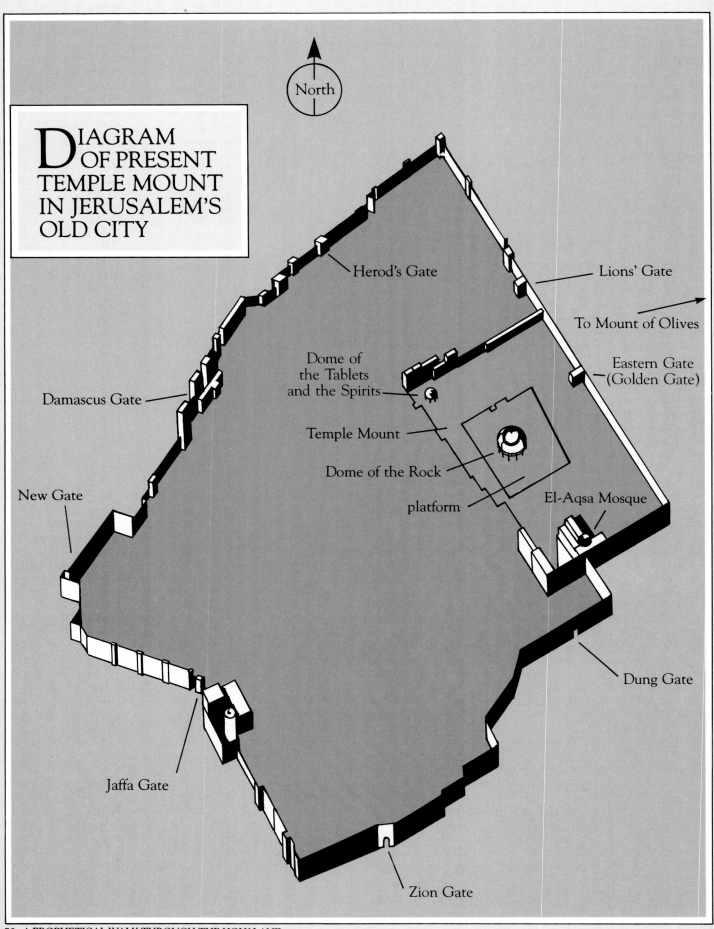

DIAGRAM OF PRESENT TEMPLE MOUNT IN JERUSALEM'S OLD CITY

North

Herod's Gate

Lions' Gate

To Mount of Olives

Dome of
the Tablets
and the Spirits

Eastern Gate
(Golden Gate)

Damascus Gate

Temple Mount

Dome of the Rock

El-Aqsa Mosque

platform

New Gate

Dung Gate

Jaffa Gate

Zion Gate

THE SECOND CLUE

I have referred to the Dome of the Tablets and the Spirits several times. It is the little cupola (see photos on pages 57, 61, and 64) that for centuries has stood unnoticed at the northwest corner of the Temple platform, just inside of the arched entrance. (The cupola's location can be seen on the chart on the facing page.) Dr. Kaufman brings out the following amazing facts about this small dome.

First, it is situated over a smooth, flat rock mass that is actually part of the bedrock of Mount Moriah. It is only one meter lower than the only other exposed bedrock of the Temple area—the Temple Mount's highest point, over which the Dome of the Rock stands.

The bedrock under the cupola (see photo on page 61) is unique in that it is flat and yet bears no evidence of having been shaped by tools. This site was obviously recognized as a holy place since no paving stones were ever placed over it, distinguishing it from the rest of the exposed Temple platform.

Second, the Moslems who originally built the Dome of the Rock complex in the eighth century gave this cupola two very important and revealing names. The first one is *Qubbat el-Arwah*, which means "the Dome of the Spirits." I believe with Dr. Kaufman that this was so named to preserve the memory of God's presence over the Mercy Seat, above the Ark of the Covenant, which sat on the flat bedrock unshaped by human hands.

The second Arabic name given to this cupola is *Qubbat el-Alouah*, which means "the Dome of the Tablets." I believe that this name was given to reverence the memory of the tablets of the Law given to Moses by the Lord on Mount Sinai and later placed inside the Ark of the Covenant.

Dr. Kaufman points out that both the *Tosefta* and the *Mishnah Yoma* 5:2 say that the Ark of the Covenant rested on a "foundation stone" inside the Holy of Holies. I believe that this evidence, taken together with the exact measurements from many archaeological reference points that Dr. Kaufman has uncovered, establishes this bedrock as one of the holiest places on earth— the place where the manifest presence of God dwelt for centuries. This was a place so holy that only the high priest could enter it once a year with the blood of a divinely prescribed sacrifice (*Leviticus 16*).

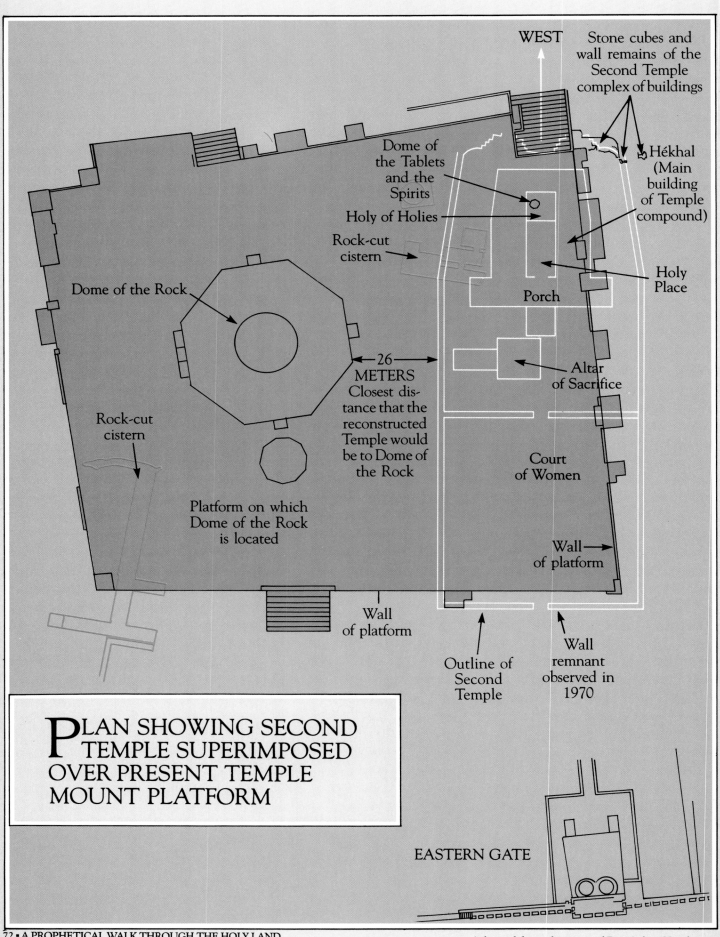

WEST

Stone cubes and
wall remains of the
Second Temple
complex of buildings

Dome of
the Tablets
and the
Spirits

Hékhal
(Main
building
of Temple
compound)

Holy of Holies

Rock-cut
cistern

Holy
Place

Dome of the Rock

Porch

26
METERS
Closest dis-
tance that the
reconstructed
Temple would
be to Dome of
the Rock

Altar
of Sacrifice

Rock-cut
cistern

Court
of Women

Platform on which
Dome of the Rock
is located

Wall
of platform

Wall
of platform

Outline of
Second
Temple

Wall
remnant
observed in
1970

PLAN SHOWING SECOND TEMPLE SUPERIMPOSED OVER PRESENT TEMPLE MOUNT PLATFORM

EASTERN GATE

Adapted from diagram of Dr. Asher Kaufman.

THE THIRD CLUE

Dr. Kaufman traced the origin of the tradition that the large rock under the Dome of the Rock was part of the ancient Temple foundation back to a Moslem Jew of the eighth century, named Wahb ibn Monabbih. Both Moslems and Christians accepted and preserved this theory, and later it was even accepted by the Jews.

However, neither one of the two main theories about just what part of the Temple was built on top of the large rock inside the Dome of the Rock can be reconciled with the exact descriptions recorded in the *Mishnah*. (The *Mishnah* is a collection of laws, regulations, and customs which governed religious practice during the period of the Second Temple. This document is the richest source of information about the Second Temple.)

One theory places the site of the Temple's Holy of Holies on the large rock. According to Dr. Kaufman, this would be just about impossible. If the Temple foundation were laid out on the Mount from this reference point, the eastern wall of the Temple would practically be on top of the eastern wall of the city, in direct contradiction of the description presented in the *Mishnah*.

Another theory is that the large rock was the site of the altar of sacrifice. According to Dr. Kaufman, this too would be impossible. He says that the steep slope to the west of the large rock would have required the construction of a massive substructure in order to support the Temple building. However, there is absolutely no evidence of such a substructure from either literature or archaeological investigation.

CLUES THAT ESTABLISHED TEMPLE LOCATION

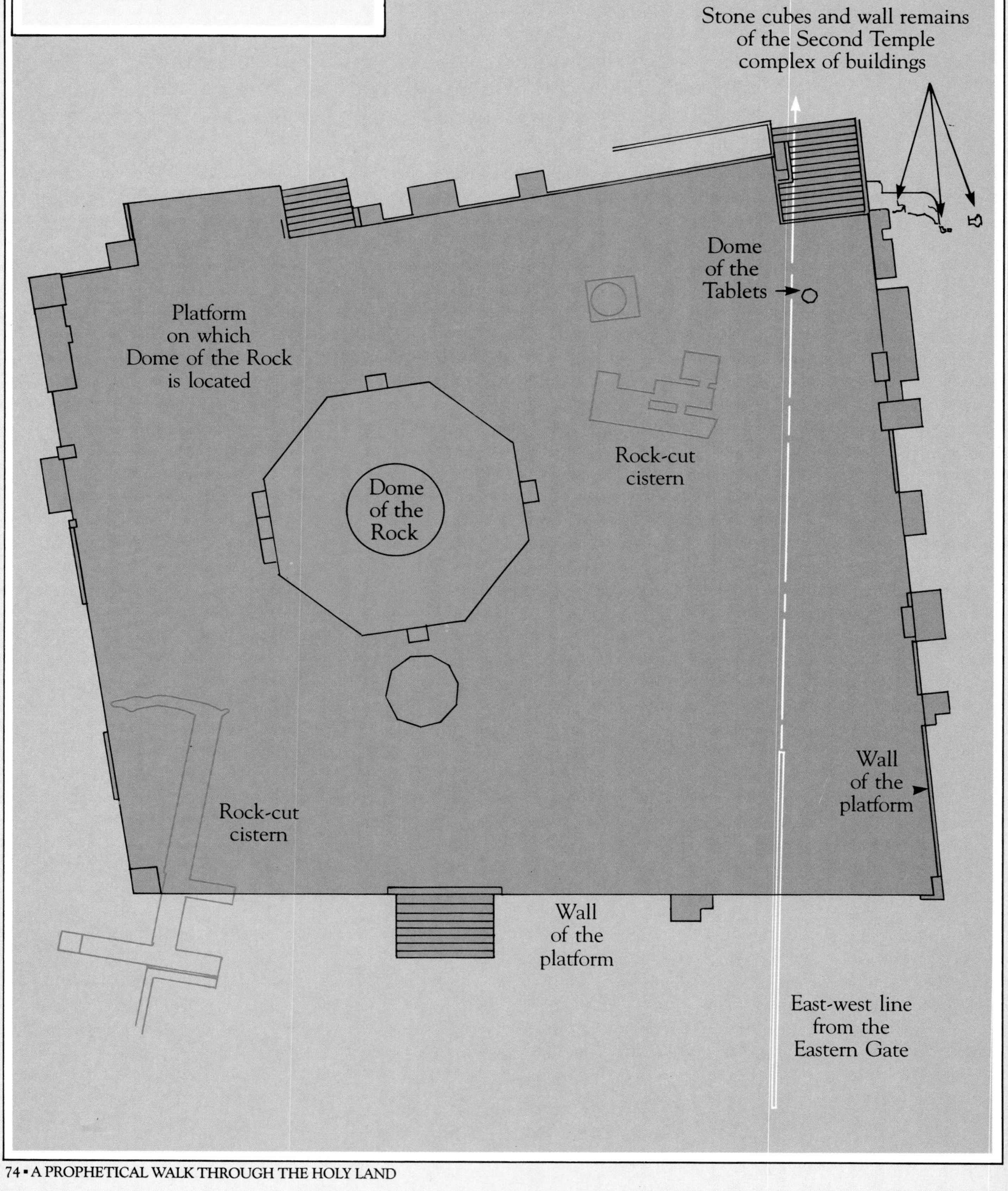

Stone cubes and wall remains of the Second Temple complex of buildings

Platform on which Dome of the Rock is located

Dome of the Tablets

Dome of the Rock

Rock-cut cistern

Rock-cut cistern

Wall of the platform

Wall of the platform

East-west line from the Eastern Gate

THE FOURTH CLUE

Once Dr. Kaufman found certain evidence on the Temple Mount, he could begin to predict the general location of specific stones and cisterns. He did this through the detailed information concerning the Temple that is contained in the *Mishnah*, the *Tosefta*, and the writings of a Jewish historian named Josephus, who lived at the time of the Second Temple's destruction. (The charts identify the various cisterns and foundation stones that were actually part of the Second Temple.) Through these lines of evidence, Dr. Kaufman had ample proof to establish the exact foundation of both the First and Second Jewish Temples.

I believe that Dr. Kaufman's dedicated and tireless investigation has provided the world with a priceless discovery.

I also believe that this discovery has accelerated the countdown to the events that will bring the Messiah Jesus back to earth. The reason for this belief is that the predicted Third Temple can now be built without disturbing the Dome of the Rock. As shown on the chart, the Temple and its immediate guard wall could be rebuilt and still be twenty-six meters away from the Dome of the Rock.

Revelation chapter 11 indicates this very situation: "I was given a reed like a measuring rod and was told, 'Go and measure the temple of God and the altar, and count the worshipers there. But exclude THE OUTER COURT; do not measure it, because it has been given to the GENTILES. They will trample on the holy city for 42 months'" (*Revelation 11:1,2 NIV*).

The outer court, which includes the area where the Dome of the Rock is situated, was given to the Gentiles. So this prophecy accurately reflects the situation that is present today.

The stage is fully set for the False Prophet of Israel and the Antichrist of Rome to be revealed to the world and initiate the construction of the Third Temple.

It is mind-boggling to realize that this piece of bedrock, which was the site of the Ark of the Covenant and God's presence, will very soon be the place where the Antichrist will take his seat and proclaim himself God (*2 Thessalonians 2:3,4*). That act, according to the Lord Jesus (*Matthew 24:15-22*), will trigger the three-and-one-half-year-long Great Tribulation and the worst war of all time.

All of these things are tremendously exciting to those who know Bible prophecy. We are literally in the very last days of the Church Age. The Temple will be rebuilt soon!

Orthodox Jews pray and read the Torah at the Western Wall. A closer inspection of the wall itself would reveal tiny pieces of paper tucked into the crevices. On them are prayers to the Almighty God who promised this land to His people.

Bethlehem's Child

"But you, Bethlehem Ephrathah, though you are small among the clans of Judah, out of you will come for me one who will be RULER over Israel, whose origins are from of old, from the days of eternity" (Micah 5:2 NIV; circa 750 B.C.).

From the day that Micah uttered the above prophecy, Bethlehem became a very special place in the plan of God. In this humble little village, the Eternal One stepped into time and became a Man. He who made the heavens and the earth voluntarily laid aside the use of His awesome divine powers to live for awhile among us as a true human being (*Philippians 2:5-8*).

Wonder of wonders, what grace was displayed here! The Word, who existed before all beginnings, who was always face to face with God, who Himself *is* God, who created all things that have come into being, became flesh and dwelt among us (*John 1:1-4*).

The amazing thing is that the Man, Jesus the Messiah, has a human mother, but no human father. God Himself is the Father of Jesus' human nature. This is why His human nature is called the Son of God—because God is His Father directly and in a unique sense.

A mother with her children on the road to Bethlehem. It was to this humble little Judean town that the promised Messiah came as a newborn Baby.

The Church of the Nativity in Bethlehem Square towers over the place where Emperor Constantine's mother, Helena, believed that Jesus was born. This basilica was constructed by Emperor Justinian (A.D. 527-565) and later altered by the Crusaders.

Bethlehem viewed from the bell tower of the Church of the Nativity. Every Christmas Eve thousands of people gather in Manger Square at the foot of this tower to celebrate the birth of Christ.

This wonderful fact is brought out in the angel's announcement of Jesus' birth to Mary: "The angel said to her: 'Do not be afraid, Mary, you have found favor with God. You will be with child and give birth to a Son, and you are to give him the name Jesus. He will be great and will be called THE SON OF THE MOST HIGH. The Lord God will give him the throne of his father David, and he will reign over the house of Jacob forever; his kingdom will never end.'

" 'How will this be,' Mary asked the angel, 'since I am a VIRGIN?' And the angel answered and said to her, 'The Holy Spirit will come upon you, and the power of the Most High will overshadow you; AND FOR THAT REASON THE HOLY OFFSPRING SHALL BE CALLED THE SON OF GOD' " (*Luke 1:30-35 NIV*).

Elizabeth, a relative of Mary, was barren, yet she miraculously gave birth at a very old age six months before Mary gave birth to Jesus. Elizabeth's child was none other than the greatest of all prophets, John the Baptist. So John was actually Jesus' cousin according to the flesh. Mary and Elizabeth met at the well pictured here and shared what the Lord had done for them. The well is located in a suburb of Jerusalem called *Ein Karem*, the birthplace of John the Baptist. (*See Luke 1:39-80.*)

Elizabeth's Well. Just about ten miles west of Old Jerusalem, this is where Mary met with Elizabeth and shared what the Lord had done for her.

Ruins of the once mighty Senate from which Caesar Augustus sent out a decree to enroll the entire Roman Empire for taxes. In the providence of God, this decree helped to fulfill the prophecy that the Messiah would be born in Bethlehem.

DIVINE PROVIDENCE IN ACTION

Many months before Mary was due to give birth, mighty Caesar Augustus in far-off Rome decided to have the entire inhabited earth enrolled in a census in order for taxes to be extracted more efficiently. Several months elapsed before his command reached the nation of Israel, located on the eastern edge of the Roman Empire. The order required every Israelite to return to the city of his forefathers because the genealogies were kept at the original site of each family's first land grant. Under Joshua the tribes and families had been assigned definite geographical territories. So for this reason, Joseph and Mary—both descended from King David—had to return to the family homestead in Bethlehem to be registered.

Caesar Augustus unwittingly issued an order that forced a very pregnant young Jewish girl to make a difficult journey from Nazareth to Bethlehem, and there she gave birth to the Messiah—in the exact place predicted hundreds of years before.

SHEPHERDS MEET THE GREAT SHEPHERD

How fitting it was for the birth of the Great Shepherd of men's souls to be first announced to humble shepherds in the fields near Bethlehem! An angel of the Lord appeared to them and said, "Do not be afraid; for behold I bring you good news of a great joy which shall be for all the people; for today in the city of David there has been born for you a SAVIOR, WHO IS THE CHRIST, THE LORD. And this will be [an identifying] sign for you: you will find a baby wrapped in clothes, and lying in a manger" (*Luke 2:10-12*).

What an incredible revelation was made to these shepherds! The Baby who had just been born in Bethlehem was the Savior of mankind, the long-awaited Messiah of the Jews, and the Lord Himself from heaven. No wonder they raced to Bethlehem and worshiped Him! All those who are blessed enough to have their eyes opened will also worship Him.

A flock of sheep graze on a hillside in Shepherds Field east of Bethlehem. Here an angel announced to astonished shepherds: *"Today in the town of David a Savior has been born to you; he is Christ the Lord" (Luke 2:11 NIV).*

Photo on following page.

Jesus' public ministry began at the Jordan River. Here His cousin John baptized Him and the Holy Spirit descended upon Him in the form of a dove (*Matthew 3:13-17*).

JESUS' BAPTISM AT THE JORDAN RIVER

Jesus officially began His public ministry at His baptism. The divinely appointed herald of the Messiah, John the Baptist, had no idea who the Messiah was, but God had told him that the Messiah was living and walking among the people, and He gave John an identifying sign. The Messiah would come to him for baptism. When He came out of the water, the Holy Spirit in the form of a dove would come upon Him (*John 1:29-34*). Imagine how shocked John must have been when he discovered that his own cousin Jesus was the Son of God and the Messiah!

A precious truth is revealed in the baptism of Jesus. John, not yet aware that Jesus was the Messiah, asked Him when He came to be baptized, "I have need to be baptized by You, and do You come to me?" (*Matthew 3:14*). This statement reveals the kind of life that Jesus led during those so-called silent years between ages twelve and thirty. Jesus' faith and walk with God was such that John the Baptist recognized Him as holier than himself. Remember that this was *before* he realized who Jesus really was!

THE UNIQUE BAPTISM

No one will ever be baptized for the reason that Jesus was baptized. The Greek word *baptized* is used metaphorically in the New Testament. The root idea means "to dip something in another substance." We use the word in that sense today; for instance, when a rookie soldier goes into combat for the first time, the experience is commonly called his "baptism of fire." This means that he is so immersed

in the experience of real war that he is changed.

Those who followed Moses out of Egypt through the Red Sea were said to be "baptized into Moses." (*See 1 Corinthians 10:1-2.*) Yet it is extremely important to note that the Israelites did not get wet, for the Bible says explicitly, "But the sons of Israel walked on dry land through the midst of the Red Sea, and the waters were like a wall to them on their right hand and on their left" (*Exodus 14:29*). The Egyptians got wet but were not baptized—they were destroyed.

The point is this: The Israelites were so *identified* with Moses' faith that they were said to be baptized into Moses with the result that their destiny and nature were changed. This gets at the true New Testament meaning of the word *baptism*.

Jesus' own baptism represented His total immersion into the Father's will. In essence He was saying to His Father, "I am ready and willing to die for man's sin, and I'm qualified to bear the burden on behalf of mankind." His Father's response was, "This is My Beloved Son in whom I am well pleased" (*Matthew 3:13-17*). He acknowledged the worthiness of His Son, Jesus, to become the substitutionary sacrifice for man's sin. John the Baptist understood this later when he saw Jesus return from His forty days of temptation in the wilderness and proclaim to the people, "Behold, THE LAMB OF GOD who takes away the sin of the world" (*John 1:29*).

A political "hot spot" since the conclusion of World War I, the Israeli War of Independence made a section of the Jordan an international frontier between Israel and Jordan. After the Six Day War in June 1967, practically the entire Jordan became the cease-fire line between the two states.

POOL OF SILOAM

The Pool of Siloam is connected to the Gihon Spring by one of the most amazing feats of engineering in the ancient world. This connecting conduit is called Hezekiah's Tunnel.

The Gihon Spring, which provided Jerusalem's main water supply, was outside the ancient lower southern walls of the city. The Pool of Siloam was inside the wall in an area called the City of David.

In 701 B.C., during the reign of King Hezekiah of Judah, a formidable Assyrian army led by King Sennacherib began to move toward Jerusalem. They had conquered the ten tribes of the Northern Kingdom of Israel twenty years earlier.

In order to protect the water supply from the invading Assyrians, and to prepare Jerusalem for a siege, King Hezekiah ordered a tunnel to be cut through solid rock to connect the outer spring with the one inside the wall. As the Assyrian army approached Judea, the men began to tunnel from both ends and miraculously met in the middle within four feet of each other. They cut a tunnel through solid rock, 1,777 feet long and an average of six feet high. Once the two pools were connected, they covered the Gihon Spring so that the Assyrian army was unaware of its existence.

As it turned out, God supernaturally delivered Jerusalem. Sennacherib sent a letter to Hezekiah that blasphemed the God of Israel. Hezekiah immediately took the letter to the Temple, laid it before the Lord and prayed a beautiful prayer of faith (*2 Kings 19:14-19*).

In response, God sent the prophet Isaiah with this answer: "Because you have prayed to Me about Sennacherib king of Assyria, I have heard you… Therefore thus says the Lord concerning the king of Assyria, 'He shall not come to this city or shoot an arrow there; neither shall he come before it with a shield, nor throw up a [siege] mound against it. By the way that he came, by the same he shall return, and he shall not come to this city,' declares the Lord. 'For I will defend this city to save it for My own sake and for My servant David's sake' " (*2 Kings 19:20, 32-34*).

God sent an angel that night who destroyed 185,000 Assyrian soldiers. Sennacherib returned to Nineveh and was soon assassinated. As Isaiah predicted, not even one arrow flew over the walls of Jerusalem.

The Gihon Spring, located outside of the city wall and vulnerable to attack, was Jerusalem's main source of water in Old Testament times. Two and a half centuries after Solomon was crowned, King Hezekiah constructed the Siloam Tunnel through solid rock to bring the Gihon's water within the city walls.

POOL OF SILOAM'S GREATER MEANING

The literal meaning of the Pool of Siloam is "the pool of the One who will be sent"—that is, the Messiah. It was regarded as a prophetic symbol of the Messiah, who would come and pour water upon the desert and the parched ground. Most important, to the Hebrews it was a symbol of the Messiah pouring the Holy Spirit upon them.

In Jesus' day the priests performed a special symbolic ritual at the Pool of Siloam on the last day of the week-long Feast of Tabernacles. On that day, which was called the Great Day of the Feast, the high priest would lead a parade of priests to the Pool of Siloam. There he would fill a special pitcher with water; and then with a great crowd of people following him, he would return to the brazen altar of sacrifice. He would pour the water upon the altar as he quoted Isaiah's prophecy of the Messiah: "For I will pour out water on the thirsty land and streams on the dry ground; I will POUR OUT MY SPIRIT on your offspring, and My blessings on your descendants…" (*Isaiah 44:3*).

Then the crowd would fall silent and pray for the Messiah to come and pour His Spirit upon them. It was at this moment that Jesus stepped out from the crowd and shouted, "If any man is thirsty, let him come to Me and drink.

He who believes in Me as THE SCRIPTURE HAS SAID, 'From his innermost being shall flow rivers of living waters.' But this He spoke of the Spirit…" (*John 7:37-39*). That day the prophetic ritual of the "pool of the One who will be sent" was fulfilled! This was Jesus' greatest and boldest claim to being the Messiah. As the people prayed for Him to come and pour out His Spirit, Jesus responded, "Here I am. Come and drink!"

At the Pool of Siloam, Jesus restored the eyesight of a man born blind (*John 9:1-6*). *Siloam* means "the One who will be sent." It was symbolic of the Messiah's coming.

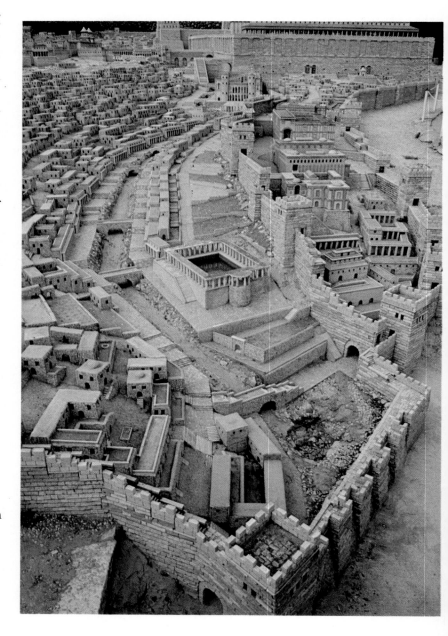

The model of New Testament Jerusalem viewed from the south shows the relationship of the Pool of Siloam (square structure at center of picture) to the Temple area.

Sea of Galilee

Jesus loved the Sea of Galilee, and some of His greatest miracles were performed in the surrounding area. Most of the apostles were originally fishermen on this sea. From these shores Jesus called them to follow Him.

I especially love the Sea of Galilee because it has remained very much the same as it was in Jesus' day—and I'm thankful it's too big for some well-meaning group to cover it with a church building!

I've often walked these shores and meditated on all that Jesus did here. This is where He borrowed Simon Peter's boat in order to preach to the multitudes on the shore. Later He amazed Simon and all his fishing partners by miraculously filling their nets with so many fish that they almost burst under the weight. While Simon, James, and John marveled at this miracle, Jesus said, "Do not fear, from now on you will be catching men" (*Luke 5:10*). From that moment they left everything and followed Him.

Twice on these shores Jesus miraculously multiplied a few loaves of bread and a few fish to feed thousands of astonished people. Twice Jesus walked upon the stormy waters of this sea. On one occasion Peter asked to be allowed to walk toward Him on the water, and Peter actually did walk on the water for a few moments. "But when Peter beheld the wind, he became afraid, and beginning to sink, he cried out, saying, 'Lord, save me!' " (*Matthew 14:30-31*). Jesus saved Peter before he went under, gently chiding him, "O you of little faith, why did you doubt?"

There's an important lesson here. As long as Peter kept his mind on the Lord, he saw Him as bigger than the threatening circumstances he found himself in. But when he shifted his

Fishermen still cast their nets into the Sea of Galilee. On one occasion, after Simon Peter and his companions had fished all night and caught nothing, the Lord instructed him to launch the boat and try again. This time when they let down the nets, they came up filled to bursting. Friends in another boat tried to help land the fish, but the catch was so heavy that both boats began to sink. Because of this miracle, Simon Peter and his fishing partners James and John *"pulled their boats up on shore, left everything and followed him* [the Messiah]" (*Luke 5:11 NIV*).

The Sea of Galilee is a large freshwater lake formed between the Galilean hills and the Golan Heights. Sixty-four square miles in area, its shores encircle nearly one hundred forty-one billion cubic feet of water.

Sometimes called Gennesaret (*Luke 5:1*) or Lake Tiberias from the resort town that Herod Antipas built on its western shore (*John 6:1; 21:1*), this harp-shaped lake is also known as Kinneret, from the Hebrew word *kinnor*, meaning "harp." The ancient rabbis used to say, "Jehovah has created seven seas, but the Sea of Galilee is His delight."

After leaving Nazareth, Jesus' Galilean ministry was centered around Capernaum, on the Sea of Galilee's northern shore. He performed a great many of His miracles here, and on a hill near Capernaum He preached the Sermon on the Mount.

Photo on following page.

A view of the Sea of Galilee. Five of the Messiah's twelve disciples came from towns around here, and four were fishermen.

focus to the storm, in his mind it became bigger than Jesus' faithfulness and power to deliver him. So down he went.

We can walk above the storms of life in the same way—as long as we keep our faith focused on Jesus, the Author and Finisher of our faith. If we dwell on our problems instead, they will appear bigger to us than the Lord's ability to handle them. The key is to cast all our cares upon Him, for He cares for us (*1 Peter 5:7*).

Many of Jesus' most startling miracles of healing were performed around this sea. Matthew records, "And departing from there, Jesus went along the Sea of Galilee, and having gone up to the mountain, He was sitting there. And great multitudes came to Him, bringing with them those who were LAME, CRIPPLED, BLIND, DUMB, and MANY OTHERS, and they laid them down at His feet; and HE

HEALED THEM, so that the multitude marveled as they saw the dumb speaking, the cripple restored, and the lame walking, and the blind seeing; and they glorified the God of Israel" (*Matthew 15:29-31*).

These miracles were Jesus' prophetic credentials which proved that He was the Messiah. They precisely fulfilled Isaiah 35:3-6, which speaks of the miracles the Messiah would perform: "Encourage the exhausted, and strengthen the feeble. Say to those with palpitating [anxious] heart, 'Take courage, fear not. Behold, your God will come with vengeance; the recompense of God will come, but He will save you.' Then the eyes of the blind will be opened, and the ears of the deaf will be unstopped. Then the lame will leap like a deer, and the tongue of the dumb will shout for joy. For waters will break forth in the wilderness, and streams in the Arabah."

Mount of the Beatitudes

An Italian convent is now located on the site where Jesus taught the "Beatitudes" and the "Sermon on the Mount." Strangely enough, the convent was constructed in 1937 with a grant from the Italian dictator Mussolini.

Here on the northern slopes above the Sea of Galilee, a few miles west of Capernaum, Jesus preached what was to become His most famous and most-often-quoted discourse. I've always been amazed by the fact that so few understand the real meaning of this message. Many people whose lives throw doubt on their Christianity have claimed, "Oh, I live by the Sermon on the Mount." The real purpose behind the Sermon on the Mount was to show the Jews just how good they would have to be in order to earn God's acceptance by keeping the Law of Moses.

This is why Jesus took the Ten Commandments and demonstrated one by one what God considers a proper keeping of the Law. For example, Jesus said, "You have heard that the ancients were told, 'YOU SHALL NOT COMMIT MURDER' and 'Whoever commits murder shall be liable to the court.' But I say to you that everyone who is angry with his brother shall be guilty before the court; and whoever shall say to his brother, 'Raca,' shall be guilty before the supreme court; and whoever shall say, 'You fool,' shall be guilty enough to go into the hell of fire" (*Matthew 5:21-22*).

Built in 1937 by a grant from the Italian dictator Benito Mussolini, this delightful Chapel of the Beatitudes marks the traditional site where Jesus preached the Sermon on the Mount. (*Matthew 5-7*).

Jesus was not giving a new law, but rather showing what God had always considered a violation of the sixth commandment, "Thou shalt not murder." God holds us accountable for the secret thoughts, motives, and desires of our heart, as well as our actual deeds. For apart from the restraints of society, justice, and conscience, God knows that we would be inclined to kill someone we hate.

Jesus went on to interpret the seventh commandment, "You have heard that it was said, 'DO NOT COMMIT ADULTERY.' But I tell you that anyone who looks at a woman lustfully has already committed adultery with her in his heart" (*Matthew 5:27-28 NIV*). Once again He showed that God requires us to keep the Law in our heart as well as in our outward behavior. He emphasized how impossible it is to keep God's standard of perfection. God's nature demands perfection; only one who is perfect can have fellowship with Him. This is why Jesus began the Sermon on the Mount by saying, 'Do not think that I have come to abolish the Law or the prophets; I have not come to abolish them, but to fulfill them" (*Matthew 5:17 NIV*). Jesus fulfilled the Law when He took upon Himself the guilt for every time we break God's standard in thought, word, or deed, *and died under our penalty.*

The Apostle Paul clarified Israel's error in trying to earn God's acceptance by keeping the Law: "Brothers, my heart's desire and prayer to God for the Israelites is that they may be saved. For I can testify about them that they are zealous for God, but their zeal is not based on knowledge. Since they did not know the righteousness that comes from God and sought to establish their own, they did not submit to God's righteousness. Christ is the end of the Law

so that there may be a righteousness for everyone who believes" (*Romans 10:1-4 NIV*). Christ brought an end to the Law of Moses because He perfectly kept its demands and died for mankind's failure to keep it. In fulfilling the Law, He removed the barrier between man and God.

In effect, God offers man two ways of approaching Him. I call these ways Plan A and Plan B. If a person asks God, "What must I DO TO EARN forgiveness and eternal life?" God will offer him Plan A. By this plan, all one has to do is keep the Law of Moses perfectly, never breaking it, as Jesus explained in the Sermon on the Mount. No one has ever been successful by this plan, but if you care to try, good luck!

However, if a person says, "I am a sinner. I can never be good enough for God to accept," God will offer Plan B: "For by grace you have been saved through faith; and that not of yourselves, it is the GIFT of God; not as a result of works, that no one should boast" (*Ephesians 2:8-9*). By Plan B we give Jesus Christ our sins and He clothes us with *His* perfect righteousness, making us acceptable to God on a just basis. Plan B doesn't set the Law of Moses aside, it fulfills it. The purpose of God's Law was to prove to us the impossibility of anyone's meriting God's approval by human effort and then to drive us to Christ, who has fulfilled the Law for us.

Whereas "religion" can only clean up outward appearances, Jesus Christ will clean up the heart and give new life with new desires and new power. Only He can produce the righteousness of the Law *within* a person. So the Lord preached the Sermon on the Mount in order to show everyone how God utterly rejects human "merit" and "religion" as a way of coming to Him for acceptance and fellowship.

A panoramic view of the Sea of Galilee from the Mount of Beatitudes. The field by the Sea is where Jesus miraculously fed five thousand men—besides women and children—with five loaves of bread and two fish (*Matthew 14:13-21*).

Capernaum

In Jesus' time, Capernaum was a thriving Jewish city of approximately ten thousand people. It was located on the north shore of the Sea of Galilee, about ten miles from Tiberias and two-and-one-half miles from where the Jordan River enters the Sea.

The Scripture says of Jesus, "And leaving Nazareth, He came and settled in Capernaum, which is by the sea, in the region of Zebulun and Nephtali" (*Matthew 4:13*). This became His "hometown" when He began His ministry. On several occasions He taught in the synagogue located on the very site where the ruins shown in the photograph stand today. Jesus taught some of His most important lessons in Capernaum. (*See Matthew 13; 15:1-20; 17:24-27; 18:1-35; Mark 2:1-28; 7:1-23; 9:33-50; Luke 6:1-5; and John 6:22-71.*)

Peter and James lived at Capernaum, and from this city Jesus called them as well as Andrew, John, and Matthew to be His disciples (*Mark 1:16-21*). Capernaum was greatly honored for another reason; it was here that Jesus chose to perform some of His greatest miracles. He delivered several men from demon possession. He healed Peter's mother-in-law, as well as thousands of other people from every kind of disease and sickness. Jesus even raised a man's daughter from the dead. (*See Luke 8:41-42, 49-56.*)

Close-up of the synagogue ruins at Capernaum, Jesus' adopted hometown on the northern shore of the Sea of Galilee.

The Messiah spent much of His time in the first-century synagogue over which this second-century building was erected.

But although so many miracles were performed in and around Capernaum, most of the people there did not believe Jesus was their Messiah. And because of their unbelief and lack of repentance, He predicted a harsh penalty on Capernaum and her sister cities, Chorazin and Bethsaida: " 'Woe to you, Chorazin! Woe to you, Bethsaida! For if the miracles had occurred in Tyre and Sidon which occurred in you, they would have repented long ago in sack cloth and ashes. Nevertheless I say to you it shall be more tolerable for Tyre and Sidon in the day of judgment, than for you. And you, Capernaum, will not be exalted to heaven, will you? You shall descend to hades, for if the miracles had occurred in Sodom which occurred in you, it would have remained to this day. Nevertheless I say to you that it shall be more tolerable for the land of Sodom in the day of judgment, than for you' " (*Matthew 11:20-24*).

The ruins of Capernaum bear eloquent testimony to the accuracy of His prophecy. The city was destroyed and even though it was in a choice location, it was never rebuilt.

Capernaum's failure offers a crucial lesson for Christians today. Many believe that physical miracles are the most important experiences to be sought by the church. They assume that if people see miracles, they will immediately put their faith and trust in the Lord and grow to spiritual maturity. But what happened to Capernaum reveals that although people saw incredible miracles performed by Christ Himself, they *still* didn't believe! This should shake us all!

Among the crumbling stones of the synagogue at Capernaum is a relief of the Ark of the Covenant being transported on a cart.

The Ark contained two tablets of the Decalogue (the Ten Commandments) which God gave to Moses at Sinai.

A star of David carved in stone remains in the rubble.

An ancient olive press at Capernaum is a vague reminder of what was once a well-populated, important city—and a city of some self-importance! Jesus asked the people here: "*And you, Capernaum, will you be lifted up to the skies? No, you will go down to the depths. If the miracles that were performed in you had been performed in Sodom, it would have remained to this day*" (*Matthew 11:23 NIV*). Capernaum was destroyed and never rebuilt.

When a Jewish royal official sought Jesus in order for Him to heal his son, Jesus said in a grieved tone, "Unless you people see signs and wonders, you simply will not believe" (*John 4:48*). When Thomas, one of the twelve disciples, said that he wouldn't believe that Jesus had been resurrected until he put his finger into the nail wounds in His hands and his hand into the wound in His side, Jesus appeared to him. *Then* Thomas exclaimed, "My Lord and my God!" The Lord's reply to him is tremendously important for us to consider today: "Because you have seen Me, have you believed? BLESSED ARE THEY WHO DID NOT SEE, AND YET BELIEVED" (*John 20:25-29*).

God much prefers us to believe because of the Holy Spirit's witness to the trustworthiness of His Word rather than because of physical miracles. This point is amplified in the biblical account of the rich man and Lazarus. The rich man died an unbeliever and went to Hades, a place of torment. When he saw Abraham off in the distance, in Paradise, he begged him to send Lazarus as a messenger from the dead to warn his family. "But Abraham said, 'They have Moses and the prophets; let them hear them.' But he said, 'No, father Abraham, but if someone goes to them from the dead, they will repent!' But he said to him, 'If they do not listen to Moses and the prophets, neither will they be persuaded if someone rises from the dead' " (*Luke 16:29-31*).

Many of the miracles recorded in Scripture accommodated people who needed to be jolted into awareness of God's power and faithfulness. However, God wants us to believe Him on the basis of His Word instead of having to witness signs and wonders. The ultimate goal of maturity in Christ is perfect faith. "Now faith is the assurance of things hoped for, the conviction of things NOT SEEN" (*Hebrews 11:1*).

God will sometimes allow us to experience hard times, trials, and even illness in order for us to exercise our faith and grow. He wants us to learn to believe Him *in spite* of our circumstances. Faith is like a muscle; unless it's exercised and stretched to the limit of its endurance, it will not grow. God wants us to do far more than what we would accomplish

A synagogue built of black volcanic rock is part of the ruins at Chorazin (or Korazin) near the Sea of Galilee. On the basalt hills above its sister city, Capernaum, this city was also denounced by Jesus (*Matthew 11:21*). Chorazin eventually died out, and very little is known about it anymore.

in perpetual comfort. He is our Leader in a spiritual battle (*Ephesians 6:10-18*), and our goal should be perfect obedience in the midst of our difficulties—not to demand that He immediately release us from the fray [trial]! "We also exult in our tribulations, knowing that tribulation brings about perseverance; and perseverance, proven character; and proven character, hope..." (*Romans 5:3-4*).

We cannot make the mistake of assuming that the presence of miracles is the standard for judging true spirituality and maturity of an individual or church, or even that the presence of miracles will cause people to believe in Jesus. The church at Corinth was not lacking in any miraculous gift (*1 Corinthians 1:7*), yet the Christians there were the most immature and carnal of which we have record. And despite the many miracles Jesus performed in Ca-

pernaum, most of the people there rejected Him.

God does work miracles in His children's lives in response to faith in His promises, but miracles should not be either the basis or the focus of faith. If God for His own good reason does not perform the miracle in your life that you think you need, don't despair. He promises that He'll never tempt you beyond what you are able to bear, and when you continue to trust Him, your faith will reap an eternal reward.

I thank God that He is working miracles of all kinds in increasing numbers today. My only concern is that they will be kept in proper perspective. God is working miracles to authenticate His message and provide for and protect His servants—but the most astounding miracle is that He is still bringing people from death to life.

The Garden of Gethsemane

The greatest battle ever fought by a human being was won in this place by our Lord Jesus Christ. It was here in the Garden of Gethsemane that the human nature of Jesus the Messiah had to choose to bear the guilt for the sins of the world and experience the just penalty of death that was our due. The cup that God the Father offered to His sinless Son was the wrath of a Holy God against the sin of all mankind.

Finite as we are, we cannot comprehend the Lord's loathing of being made sin. It was not the physical suffering that He shrank from, but the prospect of being separated from God the Father and God the Spirit because of our sins. When Jesus prayed, "Father, if Thou art willing, remove this cup from Me, yet not My will, but Thine be done" (*Luke 22:42*), He used the first-class conditional clause in the original Greek. This means that Jesus knew that the Father was willing. The intensity of the battle is here brought into full view. Jesus' human nature was saying, "I wish it were possible not to go through with this, yet not My will, but Yours be done."

Jesus knew all the things that were coming upon Him. He knew that the unleashed fury of a just God against the sins of the entire human race was going to be poured upon Him. As Jesus prayed among these olive trees, He actually sweat blood because of the intense emotional and psychological strain of making His decision. Yet He freely chose to die in your place and in mine. Once the choice was made, He never wavered.

From Jerusalem's wall overlooking the Kidron Valley, we see the Garden of Gethsemane and the Church of All Nations. It was in the Garden that the future of the world was determined. The instant that Jesus voluntarily chose to go to death on the cross, the war over sin and death was won. He carried out His resolve to the very end.

The Roman Catholic Church of All Nations (or the Basilica of the Agony) is adjacent to the Garden of Gethsemane. Dedicated by the Franciscans in 1924, this basilica shelters a massive rock thought to be the place where Jesus prayed to His Father before the crucifixion.

When Jesus rose from prayer, He could see the torches of the army, guided by Judas Iscariot, coming to arrest Him. They wound their way across the Kidron Valley from the walled city. He had ample time to escape, but He had already chosen not to.

Another startling thing took place in the Garden of Gethsemane when the soldiers sought to arrest Jesus. The Scripture says, "Judas then, having received the Roman cohort, and officers from the chief priests and the Pharisees, came there [to the Garden of Gethsemane] with lanterns and torches and weapons. Jesus therefore, knowing all things that were coming upon Him, went forth, and said to them, 'Whom do you seek?' They answered Him, 'Jesus the Nazarene.' He said to them, 'I AM.' And Judas also who was betraying Him, was standing with them. When therefore He said to them, 'I AM,' they drew backward [literally, they were knocked on their backs], and fell to the ground" (John 18:3-6).

It is extremely important to understand the magnitude of what happened here. A Roman cohort is equal to a battalion of soldiers. This means that there were approximately six hundred men present. A large number is also indicated by the fact that the word for the cohort's commander in John 18:12 is Chiliarch, which means a commander of one thousand men and is equal to the position of general today.

When this Chiliarch, including the many officers from the Jews, insolently said they were after Jesus the Nazarene, Jesus responded with His ancient, sacred name that He, in His divine nature, had first spoken to Moses from the burning bush. (See Exodus 3:1-15.) The instant that He uttered "I AM" (or Yahweh, in Hebrew), such power was released that every man in the Garden was knocked off his feet and flung backward. Just picture this scene—hundreds of soldiers and officers knocked on their backs by an invisible release of divine power!

God taught this group a lesson. You don't take the Creator of the universe captive unless He permits it! Before Jesus allowed anyone to get up, He asked, " 'Whom do you seek?' And they said, 'Jesus the Nazarene.' Jesus answered, 'I told you that I am He; if therefore you seek Me, let these go their way,' that the word might be fulfilled which He spoke, 'Of those whom Thou hast given Me I lost not one' " (John 18:7-9; predicted in John 17:12).

Imagine, Jesus dictated the terms of His arrest! In essence He was saying, "If you want Me, you will let My disciples go free." Since they were all on their backs anyway, they listened.

It is said that some of the magnificent old olive trees in the Garden of Gethsemane date back to the time of Christ. Valuable for its heavy yield of olives and the ability to grow where practically no other tree can, the olive tree is one of the amazing blessings of the Promised Land. Hosea 14:6 prophesies of Israel, "His splendor will be like an olive tree..." NIV).

The Incredible Prophecy of Betrayal

Over five hundred years before Jesus was born, God instructed Zechariah to prophesy: "And I [God speaking] said to them [Israel], 'If it is good in your sight, give Me My wages; but if not, never mind!' So they [Israel] weighed out THIRTY SHEKELS OF SILVER as My wages. Then the LORD said to me, 'THROW IT TO THE POTTER, that magnificent price at which I [the Lord] was valued by them [Israel].' So I took the thirty shekels of silver and THREW THEM TO THE POTTER IN THE HOUSE OF THE LORD" (*Zechariah 11:12-13*).

There are three distinct factors to this astonishing prophecy. First, God said there would come a time when Israel would calculate His worth at thirty shekels of silver. When Judas betrayed Jesus the Messiah, the priests decided the deed was worth thirty shekels of silver (*Matthew 26:14-16*).

Second, when Judas saw that Jesus was condemned to death, he felt remorse and tried to return the silver, confessing that he had betrayed innocent blood. The chief priests insulted him and scoffed, "What is that to us?" In a rage, Judas *threw the thirty silver shekels down in the house of the Lord* (*Matthew 27:3-5*).

Third, the chief priests picked up the thirty shekels and piously said that since it was the price of blood, it wasn't lawful to put it in the Temple. So *they decided to buy a Potter's Field* as a burial place *for the poor and for strangers* (*Matthew 27:6-10*). The Potter's Field became known as the "Field of Blood," or *Hakeldama* in Aramaic. It is the valley of Gehenna south of the city walls. (*See Acts 1:18-19.*)

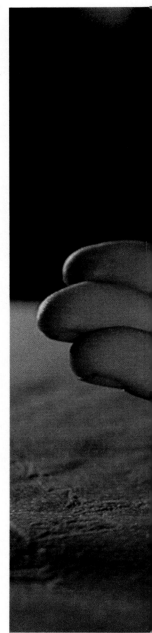

Thirty pieces of silver was the price paid for the betrayal of Jesus, the Messiah, fulfilling Zechariah's prophecy made five hundred years before His birth (*Zechariah 11:12-13*).

The Judgment of Jesus

After Jesus' arrest in the Garden of Gethsemane, He was subjected to six trials, every one of which was a mockery of justice. At His sixth trial (the second trial before Pilate), by threatening to cause trouble with Caesar, the chief priests forced Pilate to condemn Jesus. This took place at the entrance to the governor's residence, called the Antonia. The site of the judgment was called the Pavement.

The stones pictured here are under the Church of Condemnation and are probably the very ones on which Jesus was condemned to crucifixion. And this is probably where the Roman soldiers played the vicious game in which they dressed the Lord up as the King of the country which He represented, pressing a crown of thorns against His brow and throwing a purple robe over His shoulders. Then they humiliated and brutalized Him to vent their anger and contempt for His country. Scratched on the pavement stone is the word *Basilicus*, meaning the Roman "game of a mock king."

Mark says, "And the soldiers took Him away into the palace that is, the Praetorium , and they called together the whole Roman cohort. And they dressed Him up in purple, and after weaving a crown of thorns, they put it on Him; and they began to acclaim Him, 'Hail, King of the Jews!' And they kept beating His head with a reed, and spitting at Him, and kneeling and bowing before Him" (*Mark 15:16-19*).

The following prophecies were graphically fulfilled here: "I gave My back to those who strike Me, and My cheeks to those who pluck out the beard; I did not cover My face from humiliation and spitting" (*Isaiah 50:6*). "He was oppressed and He was afflicted, yet He did not open His mouth; like a lamb that is led to the slaughter, and like a sheep that is silent before its shearers, so He did not open His mouth. By oppression and judgment He was taken away; and as for His generation, who considered that He was cut off out of the land of the living, for the transgression of my people to whom the stroke was due" (*Isaiah 53:7-8*).

Golgotha, the "Place of the Skull"

This chilling photograph clearly brings out the skull on the face of the hill where many believe Jesus the Messiah was crucified. This hill is part of Mount Moriah and overlooks the same road that led to Jericho and Damascus in New Testament times. The appearance and location of the hill corresponds precisely with the biblical description. I believe that this is the place where the Messiah stood in the breach between heaven and hell, and by dying in our place made it possible for all mankind to receive a free gift of pardon.

Photo on previous page.

The Pavement, site of Jesus' sixth trial, was at the entrance to the governor's residence. The stones shown here are probably the ones on which He stood when condemned to die.

Golgotha

After His brutal beating at the hands of the soldiers, Jesus was marched out to the dreaded place called *Golgotha.* The Apostle John records the events: "They took Jesus therefore, and He went out, bearing His own cross, to the place called the Place of a Skull, which is called in Hebrew, GOLGOTHA; where they crucified Him, and with Him two other men, one on either side, and Jesus in-between. And Pilate wrote an inscription also, and put it on the cross. And it was written, 'JESUS THE NAZARENE, THE KING OF THE JEWS.' Therefore this inscription many of the Jews read, for the place where Jesus was crucified was near the city; and it was written in Hebrew, Latin, and in Greek" (*John 19:17-20*).

Even the noisy Arab bus station below Gordon's Calvary and the Moslem cemetery above it cannot erase the memory of what happened here two thousand years ago.

There is some dispute over the location of Golgotha and the Garden Tomb. For many centuries the site of both the crucifixion and the burial was believed to be within the Church of the Holy Sepulchre, which was founded by Emperor Constantine's mother, Helena, in A.D. 335 and rebuilt several times. The site pictured here was discovered by the British General Charles Gordon (the conqueror of Khartoum) in 1885. I am sure that arguments about the actual site of the crucifixion could go on endlessly without resulting in a definite conclusion. But I believe that even if this is not the site, it *is* an exact replica of the place so vividly described in Scripture:

■ The hill is located outside the city walls.

■ It overlooks the ancient main road to Jericho and Damascus.

■ It has a skull-like figure on its face.

■ It is less than one hundred fifty meters from a tomb hewn from a solid rock cliff. (More will be said about this in the next vignette.)

■ It is part of the original Mount Moriah, where Abraham offered his son Isaac as a sacrifice and God provided a substitute.

By the time Jesus was led from Fortress Antonia to be crucified, His face was so severely beaten that it no longer looked human. Luke records that the women lamented over Jesus when they saw Him (*Luke 23:27-31*). This fulfilled Isaiah's prediction: "Just as many were astonished at you, my people, so His appearance [face] was marred more than any man, and His form [body] more than the sons of men" (*Isaiah 52:14*).

Here are just a few of the many prophecies that were fulfilled in Jesus' crucifixion:

■ Jesus was crucified instead of being stoned to death, the usual Jewish method of execution. This fulfilled King David's prophecy concerning the Messiah—more than one thousand years before the crucifixion and approximately eight hundred years before crucifixion was introduced as a means of execution. Consider this perfect description of one being crucified under Israel's hot sun: "I am poured out like water, and all My bones are out of joint; My heart is like wax; it is melted within Me. My strength is dried up like potsherd, and My tongue cleaves to My jaws [in thirst]; and Thou dost lay Me in the dust of death. For dogs have surrounded Me; a band of evildoers has encompassed Me; THEY PIERCED MY HANDS AND MY FEET" (*Psalm 22:14-16*).

■ The soldiers did not want to ruin Jesus' seamless tunic, so they cast lots for it at the foot of the cross. This fulfilled another prophecy in this same Psalm: "They divide My garments among them, and for My clothing they cast lots" (*Psalm 22:18*).

■ Jesus Himself predicted that one of Isaiah's prophecies would be fulfilled in His death: "For I tell you, that this which is written must be fulfilled in Me, 'AND HE WAS CLASSED AMONG CRIMINALS'; for that which refers to Me has *its* fulfillment" (*Luke 22:37*). Jesus was quoting from Isaiah 53:12, which was prophesied more than seven hundred fifty years before His birth. This was literally fulfilled when Jesus was crucified between two criminals.

■ In this same passage, Isaiah prophetically describes the Messiah's sufferings as though He were standing by Golgotha at the foot of the cross. Listen to what the Holy Spirit foresaw through him: "He was despised and forsaken of men, a Man of sorrow, and acquainted with grief; and like one from whom men hide their face, He was despised, and we did not esteem Him. Surely our griefs He Himself bore, and our sorrows He carried; yet we ourselves esteemed Him stricken, smitten of God, and afflicted. But He was pierced through for our transgressions, He was crushed for our iniquities; the chastening for our well-being fell upon Him, and by His scourging we are healed. All of us like sheep have gone astray, each of us has turned to his own way; but the Lord has caused the iniquity of us all to fall on Him" (*Isaiah 53:3-6*).

Isaiah clearly explains *why* Jesus the Messiah died. All our sins were put upon Him, and then God judged Him in our place. When you accept that Jesus the Messiah did this for you personally, you receive forgiveness and eternal life.

Photo on following page.

The Holy City, altar of Judaism, Christianity, and Islam, is the focal point of Israel. For the past four thousand years the city has struggled through violent turmoil, belying its name, which means "Peace." According to prophetic Scripture, Jerusalem's worst years are still to come. Not until the Prince of Peace returns will the city experience harmony and security.

The entrance to the Tomb of the Kings (or Tombeau Des Rois) illustrates how a round rock was rolled into place to seal the tomb. (Note the huge stone disk just to the right of the opening.) This particular tomb is of Queen Helena, a wealthy Mesopotamian queen who moved to Jerusalem about A.D. 45.

Photo on previous page.

"…Joseph of Arimathea asked Pilate for the body of Jesus. Now Joseph was a disciple of Jesus, but secretly because he feared the Jews. With Pilate's permission, he came and took the body. He was accompanied by Nicodemus, the man who earlier had visited Jesus at night. Nicodemus brought a mixture of myrrh and aloes…

"Taking Jesus' body, the two of them wrapped it, with the spices, in strips of linen. This was in accordance with Jewish burial customs. At the place where Jesus was crucified, there was a garden, and in the garden a new tomb, in which no one had ever been laid. Because it was the Jewish day of Preparation and since the tomb was nearby, they laid Jesus there" (John 19:38-42 NIV). This tomb, located in a quiet garden near Skull Hill, fits the biblical description of the Lord's burial and resurrection.

The Garden Tomb

Not more than one hundred meters from the site of Golgotha is this ancient tomb hewn out of a solid rock cliff. It is in a garden which dates back to the era of Jesus the Messiah.

A cistern and a network of irrigating channels were excavated at the site, proving that it was an ancient garden. A dedicated society of Christians has secured the site and restored the gardens. It is now a lovely, peaceful place where pilgrims can meditate and worship the risen Lord Jesus.

The same factors noted about Golgotha apply to this site. If this is not the exact place from which the Lord Jesus was raised from the dead, then it is a perfect facsimile of the one described in the Bible.

The Apostle John described the situation as follows: "At the place where Jesus was crucified, there was a GARDEN, and in the garden a NEW TOMB, in which no one had ever been laid. Because it was the Jewish day of preparation and since the tomb WAS NEARBY they laid Jesus there" (John 19:41-42 NIV). Mark adds that the tomb was cut out of rock and that a very large stone was rolled into the front of the tomb's entrance to seal it (Mark 15:46–16:4).

To sum it up, the following factors relating to this site coincide exactly with the biblical description:

■ It is outside of the city's northern wall which was nearest the place where Jesus was condemned.

■ It is on the side of the ancient main road northward which led to Jericho and Damascus, so that many could read the death sentence on Jesus' cross. (Roman executions were customarily done at places where the most citizens would pass yet far enough away so that the stench would not overpower the city.)

■ This tomb is very near the place of crucifixion.

■ The tomb is located in an ancient garden.

■ The tomb is hewn out of solid rock.

■ A channel for the large, round stone that sealed the tomb is cut out of the rock in front of the tomb.

Photo on following page.

Wrapped mummy-like from head to foot and anointed for burial, Jesus' body was laid in an empty tomb. A massive stone was pushed across the entrance and secured by the seal of Caesar. Roman legionaries stood guard. If anyone were to break the seal, both the offender and the guards would be condemned to death by Roman law.

Jesus was dead. Every precaution was taken to prevent His followers from stealing and hiding His body. But God is a God of miracles. Death and the grave could not hold Him.

JESUS PREDICTS HIS OWN RESURRECTION

Neither Buddha, Mohammed, Krishna of the Hindus, nor any other religious leader ever predicted his own bodily resurrection and staked the validity of everything he taught, lived, and died for on its literal fulfillment. Jesus predicted that He would soon be executed and that on the third day He would be raised physically from the dead (*Mark 8:31 and 9:31*). He not only made this prophecy before His disciples, but before His bitterest enemies.

When the religious leaders and teachers demanded from Jesus a sign from heaven to prove His claim of being the Messiah, He gave them the sign of His own physical resurrection to occur three days after His death (*Matthew 12:38-40*). On this prophecy Jesus staked the validity of His whole message and mission. No other religious leader has ever made such a claim, especially to his most vehement enemies whom he knew would do anything possible to discredit him.

After Jesus' death, the first thing these religious leaders did was to go to Pilate and secure His body in the grave so that no fake resurrection could be pulled off (*Matthew 27:62-66*). These desperate men took every precaution to see that the body remained in the tomb. Pilate stationed battle-hardened Roman legionaries, who knew that failure on watch meant instant execution, to guard the tomb. In a maximum-security case such as this, sixteen soldiers per watch was normal. A stone weighing in excess of one-and-a-half tons was rolled into place along the prepared channel. The seal of Caesar was placed on the stone, warning any would-be grave robber of certain execution for breaking the seal.

In spite of every effort humanly possible, the tomb was found empty on the third day. And to add to the dilemma of the shocked religious leaders, Jesus' grave wrappings were found in the most extraordinary and impossible condition to explain.

Jesus' body was wrapped like a mummy from neck to feet with one-inch strips of linen coated with more than one hundred pounds of myrrh and aloes. Myrrh is much like shellac in consistency. (*See John 19:38-42.*) When this dried on Jesus, it formed a perfect cocoon of His body. In the resurrection, Jesus' body miraculously passed right through the wrappings, leaving them in the exact shape of His body—only empty.

This evidence of the intact grave clothes was so obviously miraculous that it brought the Apostle John to faith in the resurrection before he understood the Old Testament prophecies concerning it (*John 20:1-9*).

The resurrection of the Lord Jesus is validated by incontrovertible evidence of every kind. Keen legal experts such as Simon Greenleaf, former head of the Harvard Law School, after carefully sifting the evidence, declared Jesus' resurrection the best-established fact of ancient history.

The highest point on the horizon, the Tower of Ascension marks the place from which Jesus ascended into heaven and to which He will return. According to Zechariah, the Mount of Olives will split along a fault line extending to both the Mediterranean Sea and the Dead Sea. The split will cross just north of the Temple area.

Framed within the middle arch shown in this photograph, the Tower of the Ascension is a gentle yet constant reminder of the Messiah's promise that He will return to rule and reign.

Tower of the Ascension

The Tower of the Ascension is the most prominent landmark on the Mount of Olives and is framed within the middle arch of the photograph. This is the exact spot from which Jesus the Messiah left these earthly scenes and ascended to heaven.

What the angels said to the disciples as they watched Him ascend is of extreme importance: "Men of Galilee, why do you stand looking into the sky? This Jesus, who has been taken up from you into heaven, WILL COME IN JUST THE SAME WAY as you have watched Him go into heaven" (*Acts 1:11*). Jesus Christ will return in the same manner and to the same spot from which He departed.

This corresponds exactly with Zechariah's prediction concerning the Messiah's coming as a conquering King: "And in that day His feet will stand on the Mount of Olives, which is in front of Jerusalem on the east; and the Mount of Olives will split in its middle from east to west by a very large valley, so that half of the mountain will move toward the north and the other half toward the south.... And it will come about in that day that living waters will flow out of Jerusalem, half of them toward the eastern sea [Dead Sea] and the other half toward the western sea [Mediterranean Sea]; it will be in summer as well as winter" (*Zechariah 14:4,8*).

Even the geology of this area confirms the nearness of the Lord's return. As amazing as it may sound, a great, unstable fault line was discovered under the Mount of Olives—at the point of Jesus' ascension and running in the lines indicated in this prophecy. When the Lord Jesus sets foot upon the Mount of Olives, this prophecy will be dramatically fulfilled. According to this prophecy, Jerusalem may well become a seaport in the Millennial Kingdom.

The Upper Room

Jesus predicted on many occasions that He was going to send the Holy Spirit to indwell and work through the disciples in a unique, new way. This new ministry of the Holy Spirit in the believers was the main thrust of His teaching at the Last Supper, which was shared in a special "upper room" in Jerusalem. (*See John 13-17.*)

One of the most important points of what has been called the Upper Room Discourse was this promise by Jesus: "I will ask the Father, and He will give you another HELPER, that He may be with you forever; that is the SPIRIT OF TRUTH, whom the world cannot receive, because it does not behold Him or know Him, but you know Him because He abides with you, and WILL BE IN YOU" (*John 14:16-17*).

Whereas the Holy Spirit was with them before, He would now be *in* them forever. Jesus spoke of the Spirit's new role as "another Helper." The word for *another* in Greek means "another of the same kind." And *helper* means "one called alongside to help and defend." The Holy Spirit will therefore be a Helper in the same way that Jesus was, only the Spirit will be inside us forever. This represented a dramatic change from the Old Testament ministry wherein the Holy Spirit only indwelt a chosen few on a conditional and temporary basis.

This is the basis of another prophetic promise. Jesus said: "Truly, truly, I say to you, he who believes in Me, the works that I do shall he do also, and greater works [in quantity] than these shall he do; because I go to the Father [and will send you the Holy Spirit]" (*John 14:12*).

When Jesus was on earth, He was the only One who was fully empowered and guided by the Holy Spirit. After He paid for sin and ascended to heaven as a glorified Man, He was able to send

The Church of the Dormition, located near Zion, houses the traditional site of the upper room where Jesus and His disciples ate their last Passover supper together. That night He passed a cup of wine to His disciples and prophesied: *"Drink from it, all of you. This is my blood of the covenant, which is poured out for many for the forgiveness of sins. I tell you, I will not drink of this fruit of the vine from now on until that day when I drink it anew with you in my Father's kingdom"* (Matthew 26:27-29).

135

Another miracle at the Upper Room?

This photograph was taken of Hal Lindsey while speaking in the upper room concerning the initial coming of the Holy Spirit upon the disciples at Pentecost (*Acts 2:1-40*). Don Mollenberg snapped this photo with an electronic flash at the moment Hal was explaining the Holy Spirit's appearance in the form of "tongues of fire."

Several amazing details appear in the picture. First, the obvious tongue of fire arching up and over Hal's head. Second, the bright light in the form of an angel by the totally boarded-up window. Third, behind the tongue of fire is a figure like a hand holding a cross.

Many experts examined the thirty-five-millimeter camera, the negative, and the print, but were unable to explain the phenomena logically.

the Holy Spirit to indwell and empower on a permanent basis all those who believe in Him. Now we are doing greater works (in quantity, not quality) because the Holy Spirit is free to work through all believers on earth, not just through Jesus' humanity.

Just before Jesus ascended to heaven He gave these promises: "Behold, I am sending forth the promise of My Father upon you; but you are to stay in the city until you are CLOTHED WITH POWER FROM ON HIGH" (*Luke 24:49*). "And gathering them together, He commanded them not to leave Jerusalem, but to wait for what the Father had promised 'Which,' He said, 'You heard of from Me; for John baptized with water, but you shall be baptized with the Holy Spirit not many days from now...you shall receive power when the Holy Spirit has come upon you; and you shall be My witnesses both in Jerusalem, and in all Judea and Samaria, and even to the remotest part of the earth' " (*Acts 1:4,5,8*).

One hundred twenty Jewish disciples waited in the city as instructed. Exactly fifty days after the Passover, the day that Jesus was crucified, there was the Jewish Feast of Pentecost. In fact, *pentecost* simply means "fifty." During that feast, the one hundred twenty Jewish believers were gathered in the same upper room in which Jesus shared the last Passover with His twelve apostles.

Suddenly "there came from heaven a noise like a violent rushing wind, and it filled the whole house where they were sitting. And there appeared to them tongues as of fire distributing themselves, and they rested on each one of them. And they were all filled with the Holy Spirit and began to speak with other tongues, as the Spirit was giving them utterance" (*Acts 2:2-4*).

In the upper room that day, the unique New Testament ministries of the Holy Spirit began and the Church was born. These one hundred twenty Jewish believers were the first to be baptized by the Holy Spirit into an eternal organic union with the body of Jesus Himself, which is the true Church (*1 Corinthians 12:12-14*).

They were also given the gift of speaking in a language they had never learned; they were filled with the Holy Spirit for power (*Romans 8:1-4; Galatians 5:16-23*); they were sealed with the Spirit (*Ephesians 1:13-14*); they were permanently indwelt by the Spirit (*Romans 8:9; 1 Corinthians 6:19*). They were also given various spiritual gifts to equip them with the abilities to perform God's plan for their lives (*1 Corinthians 12*).

Hal beneath the tightly boarded windows of the upper room. The massive building erected over this important site dates back to the fourteenth century A.D. The original Byzantine church located here was destroyed and later rebuilt by the Franciscans. Changing hands again, the Church of the Dormition became a mosque to the Prophet David. In 1948, the structure was returned to the Israelis, who treasure it as the site of King David's tomb.

Akko or Acre

Akko was an important seaport dating back to 2000 B.C. It was first established by the Canaanites and later inhabited by the Phoenicians. It sits on the northern end of the same bay where modern Haifa is located. This natural harbor is at the western entrance to the fertile valley of Jezreel, or as it is known in future prophecy, the valley of Armageddon.

Many famous men of ancient history fought for and conquered Akko. Thutmose III, Seti I, and Ramses II are among the conquerors from Egypt. Sennacherib, Esarhaddon, and Ashurbanipal conquered it at different times for Assyria. Even the Egyptian queen Cleopatra held it for a time. Alexander the Great conquered and renamed it Ptolemais in 331 B.C. This was its name when the Apostle Paul visited there (*Acts 21:7*).

Israeli fishing boats port at Akko, in the Haifa Bay. A Phoenician/Hellenistic community, Akko's pagan influences led to rabbinical disputes over whether or not it should be included in the "Holy Land." At the close of the Apostle Paul's third missionary journey (A.D. 57), he stopped at Akko, then called Ptolemais, to visit with the Christian fellowship that had sprung up among the Jews there (*Acts 21:7*).

A LESSON IN DIVINE PROVIDENCE

Akko provides us with a "modern" demonstration of divine providence. Napoleon laid siege to Akko in A.D. 1798 after successfully conquering Egypt and Joppa. Akko was the last stronghold of the Turks. Had he conquered Akko, all of Palestine would have been his.

Napoleon sent his cannons by ship from Alexandria to meet him at Caesarea because of the difficulty of transporting them across the Sinai desert. He only took a few cannons with him. But British Admiral Nelson captured the French ships and Napoleon's cannons! Then, while Napoleon was fighting his way to Akko, Admiral Nelson quickly took the captured cannons to the city and turned them over to the Turks.

Finally Napoleon and his mighty army was ready to siege Akko. He placed artillery on the hill which to this day is called Napoleon's Hill (shown in the photograph). Imagine his surprise and chagrin to learn that the Turks were armed with French cannons. His own guns were turned against him!

Napoleon's artillery bombarded Akko from this hill east of the city. Ever since the French emperor's aborted attempt to conquer the ancient seaport in 1798, this hill has been dubbed Napoleon's Hill.

But there were more complications for the great military strategist. Before he got to Akko, Napoleon did not know that the Turks had fortified the city with two moats and two walls, one inside the other. The French lost many soldiers in breaching the first wall because of inadequate artillery. When Napoleon discovered that there was a *second* moat and wall, he gave up the conquest of Palestine altogether and retreated to Egypt.

The divine providence in the French army's failure to conquer Akko was this: Napoleon had promised the Jews that when he conquered Palestine, he would establish the State of Israel and give it to them. Had this occurred in 1798, it would have completely thrown off the prophetic timetable for Christ's return, for according to prophecy, the rebirth of the State of Israel is the key sign to a whole scenario of events that indicate Jesus Christ's imminent return.

The double walls and moats that defeated Napoleon became part of the national prison maintained at Akko during the British mandate. Hundreds of Jewish freedom fighters were imprisoned and executed here. Now in Israeli hands, Akko is being restored as the only model Crusader town in the Holy Land.

This is one of the cannons that British Admiral Nelson captured from a French ship en route from Alexandria and transported to the Turks at Akko. Admiral Nelson's quick thinking enabled the Turks to turn Napoleon's own guns against him!

At right is the Khan (or Caravanserai), a quadrangle constructed by the Crusaders at Akko as quarters for knights and their horses. Even after so many centuries, the Caravanserai still retains its distinctive medieval atmosphere.

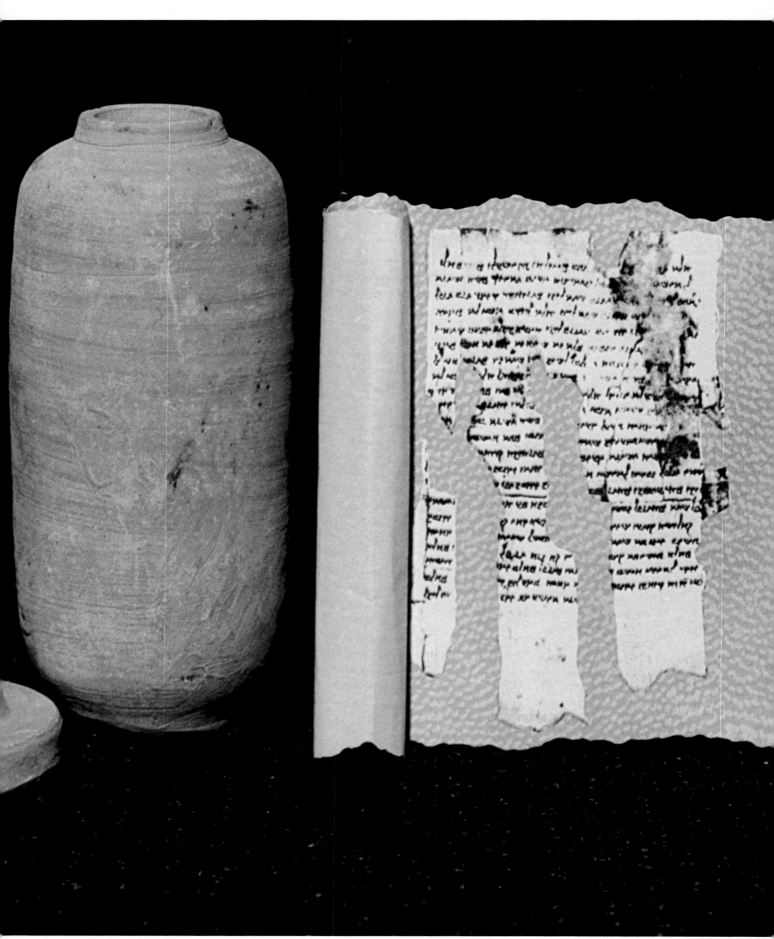

Qumran

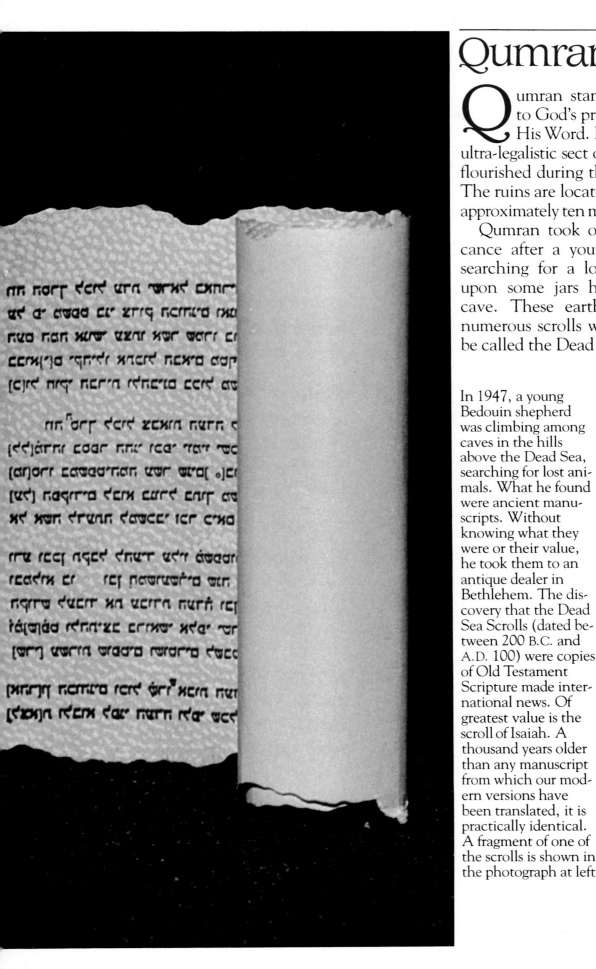

Qumran stands as a monument to God's providential care over His Word. It is a place where an ultra-legalistic sect of Jews called *Essenes* flourished during the first century A.D. The ruins are located by the Dead Sea, approximately ten miles south of Jericho.

Qumran took on particular significance after a young Arab shepherd, searching for a lost sheep, stumbled upon some jars hidden in a nearby cave. These earthen jars contained numerous scrolls which have come to be called the Dead Sea Scrolls.

Photo on following page.

In 1947, a young Bedouin shepherd was climbing among caves in the hills above the Dead Sea, searching for lost animals. What he found were ancient manuscripts. Without knowing what they were or their value, he took them to an antique dealer in Bethlehem. The discovery that the Dead Sea Scrolls (dated between 200 B.C. and A.D. 100) were copies of Old Testament Scripture made international news. Of greatest value is the scroll of Isaiah. A thousand years older than any manuscript from which our modern versions have been translated, it is practically identical. A fragment of one of the scrolls is shown in the photograph at left.

Ruins of the desert community at Khirbet Qumran. These ruins, located near the caves where the Dead Sea Scrolls were found, also became famous when a room for copying manuscripts was excavated.

The Jewish sect of Essenes who lived here wrapped their leather scrolls of the Scriptures in linen and kept them in clay jars. This ancient way of storing treasures emphasizes the priceless value of the Messianic Gospel that is stored in living "jars of clay": *"For God who said, 'Let light shine out of darkness,' made his light shine in our hearts to give us the knowledge of the glory of God in the face of Christ. But we have this treasure in jars of clay* [our human bodies] *to show that this all-surpassing power is from God and not from us"* (2 Corinthians 4:6-7 NIV).

Of all the books eventually discovered there, the scroll of Isaiah is the most valuable. The Essenes apparently had a special reverence for the scroll of Isaiah. Although the manuscript is more than one thousand years older than any known manuscript of Isaiah, it is virtually the same, word for word.

This has given great authenticity to the Book of Isaiah, which contains more prophecy concerning the Messiah than any other Old Testament book. Because of the evidence provided by the Dead Sea Scrolls, we can be certain that the incredible prophecy about the Messiah contained in the fifty-third chapter (which was so obviously fulfilled in Jesus) was indeed written hundreds of years before the events took place.

Some recent "scholars" have tried to teach that both John the Baptist and Jesus got their ideas from spending time with the Essenes. This reveals gross ignorance of both the Essene doctrines and those taught by Jesus. For instance, the Essenes were so "holier-than-thou" in their beliefs that if one of them so much as accidentally touched someone outside of the Qumran community, he would be considered ceremonially "un-

Hal views the marly cliffs where the Qumran Essenes hid their Old Testament scrolls from the Roman legionaries marching down the Jordan Valley in A.D. 68.

clean" for weeks and have to undergo elaborate cleansing rituals to be reaccepted. In contrast, Jesus constantly circulated among people the Essenes would have labeled "sinners." Jesus touched lepers as well.

The Essenes were, in fact, "super Pharisees." And we all know how much the Pharisees loved Jesus! No, the Lord Jesus didn't need any help from the Essenes for His teaching. Jesus declared very clearly from whence His teaching came: "The Jews therefore were marveling, saying, 'How has this man become learned, having never been educated?' Jesus therefore answered them, and said, 'My teaching is not Mine, but His who sent Me. If any man is willing to do His will, he shall know of the teaching, whether it is of God, or whether I speak from Myself' " (John 7:15-17).

Jesus stated and demonstrated that His teaching came from God and not man. Those who dispute this and say it came from the Essenes do so more in an attempt to discredit the Lord Jesus and His teachings than from careful analysis of the Essenes' separatist and legalistic doctrines, the very essence of which clashes with Jesus and His Word.

The ruins of the Qumran settlement are on a rocky plateau south of Jericho, overlooking the northwestern shore of the Dead Sea.

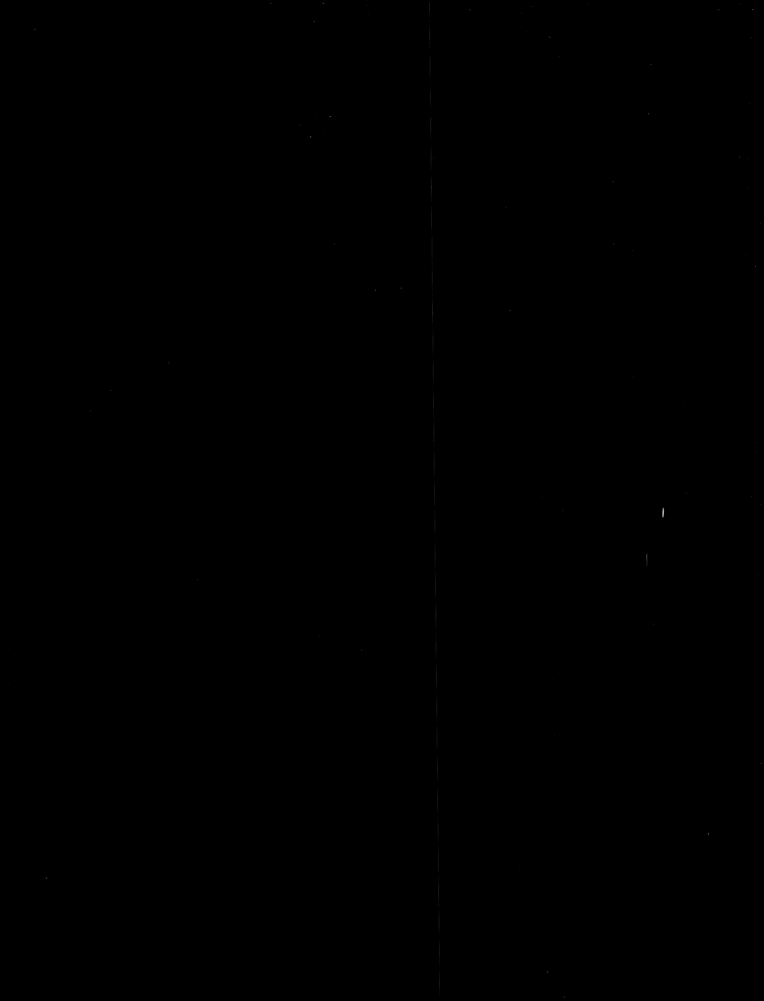

Reached by descending the Wadi Musa and passing through the mile-long Síq gorge, the city of Petra is situated in a basin surrounded by rose-red sandstone mountains. One of the most magnificent buildings chiseled out of the perpendicular rock cliffs is the Treasury, as glimpsed through the narrow entrance shown here.

The Petra Treasury.
The ancient Naba-
teans, originally of
North Africa, carved
magnificent tombs
and facades out of
Petra's beautifully
variegated red rock.

*Photo on
following page.*

This narrow canyon
with nearly touching
walls makes the Petra
basin practically
impregnable.

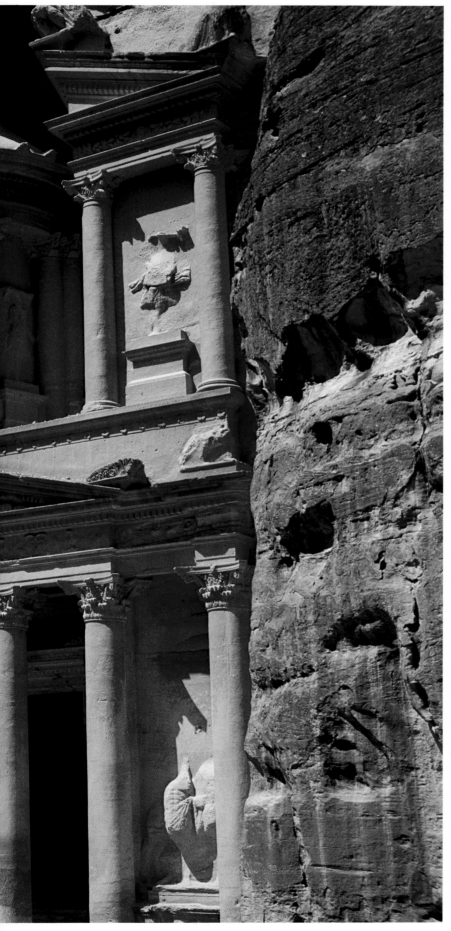

Petra

Petra in Greek means "large rock or rock cliff." The city of Petra is well-named, for all of its buildings are carved out of the beautiful rose-red rock cliffs that are native to the mountains of Edom in southern Jordan.

The site is approximately fifty miles south of the Dead Sea and is situated in the Wadi Musa Canyon. Surrounded on all sides by the rugged mountains of Edom, Petra is a formidable natural fortress because it has only one narrow entrance, a two-mile-long gorge with cliffs towering three hundred feet or more on both sides. It is less than eight feet wide in many places. The photo on page 162 shows the narrow entrance as it opens into the valley and a view of the unique building commonly called the Treasury.

No doubt this city was originally built because it was easy to defend against the various invaders continually sweeping through the Middle East. It was also in a strategic position to control the main caravan route connecting Africa and Arabia with Damascus. The Nabateans of North Africa were attracted to this location in approximately 300 B.C. They carved out the city of Petra and cheerfully proceeded to plunder the rich caravans traveling through. Later on, the Nabateans stopped robbing and simply exacted high tolls from the caravans for safe passage. They prospered and eventually extended their kingdom northward as far as Damascus. Petra was a well-known and wealthy Nabatean city during Jesus' lifetime. When the Apostle Paul was converted in Damascus, the city was ruled by a Nabatean governor.

The Romans conquered Petra in 106 A.D. and greatly enlarged it. They carved out an amphitheater, baths, shops, and homes that resemble modern condominiums. It is estimated that more than seven thousand people lived in the city during that period. Afterward the city was conquered by the Byzantines, the Crusaders, and the Moslems. The Moslems closed the city to all "infidels" until 1812. In that year an English explorer posing as a Moslem sneaked into that city which had been lost to the Western world for so long. Eventually the city was opened to visitors. Even now, everyone who visits Petra is astounded by its artistic and engineering marvels.

PETRA'S DESTINY

I believe with many other students of Bible prophecy that Petra's greatest significance is yet to come. Throughout the centuries many have believed that this is the place to which Jesus referred when He warned the inhabitants of Judea to flee to the mountains for safety. Jesus warned, "Therefore when you see the ABOMINATION OF DESOLATION which was spoken of through Daniel the prophet, standing in the holy place (let the reader understand), then let those who are in Judea flee to the MOUNTAINS; let him who is on the housetop not go down to get the thing out of the house; and let him who is in the field not turn back to get his cloak. But woe to those who are with child and to those who nurse babes in those days! But pray that your flight may not be in the winter, or on a Sabbath; for then there will be a great tribulation, such as has not occurred since the beginning of the world until now, nor ever shall" (*Matthew 24:15-21*).

In A.D. 106, Petra
came under the
jurisdiction of Rome,
evidence of which
can be seen in ruins of
baths, a central paved
street, and various
other public build-
ings, including the
impressive amphithe-
ater shown here.

Situated high on a mountain at the northern end of Petra, Temple El-Dier is part of the only remaining ruins of the original Edomite settlement, the last reminder of a vanished civilization.

The Abomination of Desolation, as touched on previously, is that event in which the Antichrist takes his seat in the Holy of Holies of the Third Temple (that will soon be built) and declares himself to be God. All believers in the area who trust in the prophetic Scriptures will heed this warning and immediately flee to Petra. It is the only place in the entire region that is secure and large enough with facilities to sustain life for an extended period of time.

The Apostle John also predicted this situation: "And when the dragon [Satan] saw that he was thrown down to the earth, he persecuted the woman [believing Israel] who gave birth to the male child [Jesus the Messiah]. And the two wings of the great eagle were given to the woman, in order that she might fly into the wilderness to her place, where she has nourished for a time and times and half a time [three and one half years], from the presence of the serpent [Satan]. And the serpent poured water like a river out of his mouth [invading armies from the USSR, Arab Union, China, and European-Roman confederacy] after the woman, so that he might cause her to be swept away with the flood. And the earth helped the woman, and the earth opened its mouth and drank up the river which the dragon poured out of his mouth [Probably an earthquake will swallow up the armies that attempt to destroy the believers hiding in Petra.]" (*Revelation 12:13-16*).

The Lord Messiah Jesus will supernaturally protect those who cling to His Word. I believe Petra will be the place of that protection.

*Photo on
following page.*

A Jordanian soldier guards the entrance to Petra.

Caesarea

This fragment of a dedication stone bearing part of the names Caesar Tiberias and Pontius Pilate was discovered in the ruins at Caesarea.

Photo on following page.

The Apostle Paul defended the gospel before King Agrippa at this amphitheater in Caesarea.

Caesarea was a very important seaport during the time of Jesus and the apostles. It is located on the Mediterranean about midway between Tel Aviv and Haifa and about seventy miles northwest of Jerusalem.

Herod built the city in honor of Caesar Augustus and spared neither money nor effort to make it a lavish, Roman-style city. It had a magnificent hippodrome, an amphitheater, a palace, and many ornate public buildings. The city also boasted Herod's surf-free harbor, an amazing feat of engineering.

As far as the Romans were concerned, Caesarea was the only bright spot in all of Israel. It was the center of Roman government for nearly five hundred years.

Many important New Testament events occurred here. Philip, the evangelist, lived and preached here, and he had four daughters who prophesied (*Acts 8:40; 21:8-9*).

Peter first brought the gospel and the new-covenant ministries of the Holy Spirit to the Gentiles in this city (*Acts 10*). This makes Caesarea extremely important to the Gentile world because before this took place, the gospel was only being preached to Jews. It was also here that the Holy Spirit was first given to non-Jews. (The Samaritans were part Jewish.)

In the early centuries, Caesarea was the home of a vital church. Missionaries were sent from here to evangelize the world. Origen established a very important school of Christian theology here in the third century A.D. Eusebius, one of the first great Christian historians, was bishop of this city from A.D. 313 to 340.

But perhaps the most important fact to remember about Caesarea is that here the Apostle Paul was imprisoned for two years after being arrested and nearly killed by the Jewish leaders in Jerusalem. Paul was specifically warned by a prophet of God named Agabus not to go to Jerusalem. But Paul went anyway, apparently out of God's will. This interesting detail is further evidenced by the fact that on this trip Paul compromised some of the principles of grace about which he had already written in the Epistle to the Galatians. (*See Acts 21:7-40.*)

Nevertheless, God worked Paul's imprisonment together for good (*Romans 8:28*). It was during this time in Caesarea that Paul's companion, Luke, gathered the information from which he wrote the Gospel of Luke. The Lord also provided for Paul's trip to Rome at Roman expense.

As a result, Paul eloquently defended the message of the Messiah Jesus before the governors Felix and Festus and before King Agrippa (*Acts 24, 25, 26*). Paul's powerful defense before King Agrippa was presented in the very amphitheater that is pictured here. The Scripture says, "And so, on the next day when Agrippa had come together with Bernice, amid great pomp, and had entered the AUDITORIUM accompanied by the commanders and prominent men of the city, at the command of Festus, Paul was brought in" (*Acts 25:23*).

Caesarea is famous for its architecture and history, but it will always be remembered especially because of the Apostle Paul's experience in this city. Here God, in His marvelous grace, caused good to result from Paul's sin of stepping out of His will.

Rome's authority was strong, and when the Jewish rebellion broke out in A.D. 66, all of the Jews at Caesarea were massacred. Earlier, the Apostle Paul was held prisoner here.

The Roman garrison city of Caesarea took twelve years to build. Although best-known for its fabulous man-made harbor, Caesarea could boast a temple in honor of Augustus Caesar (the first Roman emperor), a drainage system, assembly buildings, a garrison of three thousand Roman troops, and an aqueduct.

Sunset viewed from the Greek island of Patmos. No doubt the Apostle John saw this scene many times. To me it dramatically illustrates John's vision of the sea turning to blood in the final terrible War of Armageddon.

Patmos

Patmos today is a beautiful little island (as the photographs show) which lies on the coast of Turkey. In the Apostle John's day, however, it was an isolated desert island used by Rome to eliminate dissidents considered dangerous to the state.

As I walked around on this lovely Greek isle, I constantly had to remind myself that in this very place the Lord Jesus Christ revealed the final destiny of the world to the Apostle John, as recorded in the Book of Revelation, or the Apocalypse.

John tells us why he was sent here to die: "I, John, your brother and fellow partaker in the tribulation and kingdom and perseverance which are in Jesus, was on the island called Patmos, BECAUSE OF THE WORD OF GOD AND THE TESTIMONY OF JESUS" (*Revelation 1:9*). John was exiled to Patmos to starve to death because at the age of ninety he was still such a tiger that Rome couldn't shut him up. Roman judges kept telling him to stop proclaiming the gospel of Jesus Christ, but because of his faithfulness to God's Word he would not stop. So rather than make a public martyr of John, Rome sent him to die a slow, unknown death on Patmos. But God miraculously kept John alive and revealed to him a detailed prophecy of the destiny of mankind and planet Earth!

There are three keys to understanding this prophetic book. First, John constantly tells us that he actually SAW and HEARD the incredible wars and global catastrophes, and that he was commanded to write about them. How could this first-century man describe the scientific wonders of the latter twentieth century? He had to illustrate them with phenomena of the first century; for instance, a thermonuclear war looked to him like a giant volcanic eruption spewing fire and brimstone.

Second, the outline of the book is given in Revelation 1:19. John was commanded to write about "the things that he had seen" (*chapter 1*), "the things which are" (*chapters 2 and 3*), and "the things which shall take place after these things" (*chapters 4 through 22*). Chapters 4 through 18 specifically detail the events of the seven-year Tribulation that immediately precedes the return of the Lord Messiah, Jesus. Chapter 19 predicts the Second Advent of Jesus, with accompanying phenomena.

Third, most figures of speech used by the Apostle John are either explained in the context or in some other book of the Bible. They can be quickly traced with the help of a good Bible concordance.

It is very important to remember the first key to the Book of Revelation, however. Much of the symbolism John used was the result of a first-century man being catapulted in God's time machine up to the end of the twentieth century, then returned to his own time and commanded to write about what he had seen and heard. The only way that John could obey that instruction was to use phenomena with which he was familiar to illustrate the scientific and technical marvels that he predicts.

Hal Lindsey teaches the outline of Revelation on location at the cave where the Apostle John wrote much of the book. Trinity Broadcasting Network filmed this lecture for a television special.

Photo on following page.

Patmos harbor viewed from the mountain-side just below the monastery pictured on page 178.

As I contemplate the isolation and remoteness of the Isle of Patmos in John's day, how ironic it seems to me that from here the rise and fall of all civilization was predicted! And all of the events that John foresaw are coming together today in the precise pattern he predicted. To emphasize the nearness of the Lord's return, I want to point out a few of the specific prophetic signs that are being fulfilled simultaneously before our eyes:

■ Israel has been reborn as a nation.

■ Jerusalem is in Jewish hands.

■ The Arab nations are united in a fanatical obsession to destroy Israel.

■ The Soviet Union has fulfilled the prophecies of the great, murderous power to the extreme north of Israel.

■ The Red Chinese are building the great army of two hundred million that will march across the dried-up Euphrates River (*Revelation 16:12*).

■ The European Common Market is now comprised of ten nations, all out of the old Roman culture (*Daniel 7:24-25; Revelation 13 and 17*).

■ World conditions are ripe for the rise of the Antichrist.

SCIENCE HAS SET THE STAGE

Scientific and technical developments have reached the point where some key prophecies of the Book of Revelation can now be fulfilled. Thermonuclear weapons can do every horrible thing that John predicts in 6:12-17 and 8:7-12. In fact, I believe that he is describing a thermonuclear war when he says, "...and something like a great mountain burning with fire was thrown into the sea; and a third of the sea became blood; and a third of the creatures, which were in the sea and had life, died, and a third of the ships were destroyed" (*Revelation 8:8-9*).

When a hydrogen warhead explodes in the sea, it looks like a great mountain laced with fire. The Soviet Union has amassed the largest nuclear-missile-firing navy in history, and the West is racing to catch up. I believe that this generation will witness the greatest naval battle of all time—as part of the War of Armageddon predicted by John.

The super computers are another relevant technical development. John foresaw the Antichrist and his cohort, the False Prophet of Israel, force all the people of the world to receive a number. Without this number, no one could buy or sell or hold a job. The prefix of this number will be 666. When in history could any dictator number every person on earth? The technology did not exist before the very recent advent of super computers. (*See Revelation 13:16-18.*)

TIME TO LOOK UP

World events viewed through the grid of Bible prophecy indicate that we are rapidly moving toward the end of history as we know it.

The good news is this: Jesus Christ has promised that He will miraculously deliver all who believe in Him from this terrible holocaust. This miraculous deliverance, called the Rapture, is the event in which the Lord Jesus will mysteriously snatch every living true Christian out of the world in a split second. As we are secretly caught up in the clouds to meet the Lord, we will be miraculously transformed from mortal to immortal. Those who are part of this event will never know physical death (*1 Corinthians 15:51-53 and 1 Thessalonians 4:15-18*).

Then we will be taken to God the Father's house to be given rewards for every act of faith we have performed in this life (*John 14:1-3*). At the end of the Tribulation period, we will return to the earth with Jesus Christ, as His bride. And then, as kings and priests, we will help Him rule the new earth (*Revelation 19:7-9; 20:6*).

I pray that everyone who reads this book will be with us on that great day when the Lord Himself descends from heaven with a shout and catches up all living believers to meet Him in the air.

In the mountains of Patmos is this monastery where the Apostle John is said to have received some of his prophetic visions. One of the most ancient manuscripts of the Gospel of John is kept here.

Megiddo and Armageddon

Megiddo was a fortified city overlooking the fertile Jezreel Valley in northern Israel. It saw continuous warfare throughout most of its active history, which extended from 4000 B.C. to around 400 B.C. Extensive archaeological excavations have uncovered twenty cities built one upon another, as various wars left the city in ruins.

The reasons for this frequent warfare are easy to find. First, Megiddo sits upon a hill which commanded the main caravan route from Egypt and Africa to ancient Phoenicia, Assyria, Babylon, and later, Persia. Second, Megiddo is located in the middle of a natural "land bridge" that connects Africa, Asia, and Europe. This land bridge begins in the north at the Bosporus, a vital narrow waterway which passes through Istanbul to the Black Sea. It extends southward through what is now Turkey, Syria, Lebanon, Israel, and Sinai. In ancient times the southern end of the land bridge began with the border of Egypt. Today it begins with that crucial sea lane, the Suez Canal.

Almost all of the would-be conquerors of the past fought to possess Megiddo because of its strategic location. When the Apostle John wrote the Book of Revelation, Megiddo was a name already well-associated with turmoil because of its strategic position on the land bridge.

The culmination of human history will take place here in the Valley of Armageddon. When nothing short of a miracle can save the amazing little nation at the vortex of this world war, Israel will turn to God in supplication and accept Jesus as her Messiah. Then God will give every Israeli supernatural power and turn the tide of the war.

For nations maneuvering for world domination, control of this key port on the Bosporus is crucial. The northern anchor of the natural land bridge connecting three major continents (Europe, Asia, and Africa), it will one day prove a temptation too hard for the bear of the north (Russia) to resist (*Ezekiel 39:1-6; Revelation 16:16*).

The brightly illuminated bridge across the Bosporus divides Turkey's largest city. Built by Emperor Constantine in A.D. 330, Istanbul became the capital of the Byzantine Empire. After the city was overthrown by the Crusaders in 1204 and the Ottoman Turks in 1453, it was eventually rebuilt as the Turkish capital. Although the capital was moved to Ankara in 1923, Istanbul remains the economic hub of Turkey.

The author's wife, Kim Lindsey, views the shores of the nineteen-mile-long Bosporus, the Turkish strait historically strategic as the only sea link between the Black Sea and the Mediterranean.

The central prophecy of the *Armageddon War* is found in Revelation 16:12-16. There are many important points to observe:

■ Armageddon is not a single battle, but a campaign or an extended war. Armageddon is described as "the war [*polemos* in Greek] of the great day of God, the Almighty" (*Revelation 16:14*). *Polemos* means an extended campaign, not just one battle.

■ Armageddon is inextricably connected with two great world movements of armies. First the awesome armies of "the Kings of the East," which will be led by Red China and number two hundred million, are mustered from east of the Euphrates. The Euphrates River, which is the ancient boundary between East and West, is then miraculously dried up by an angel of God. This facilitates the Chinese armies' invasion of the Middle East (*Revelation 16:12*). Second, Satan, the Roman Antichrist, and the Jewish False Prophet use demonic deception to gather the rest of the armies from "the whole world" to counter the invasion from the East.

■ The vortex of this war to end all wars will be in the valley below Megiddo, which is prophetically called the Valley of Armageddon (*Revelation 16:16*).

THE SEQUENCE OF BATTLE

The final war begins in the middle of the Tribulation when the "Abomination of Desolation" is set up in Jerusalem's Third Temple.

The following four maps illustrate the stages of the Armageddon campaign, from the mobilization of the world's armies against Israel to the miraculous conversion and deliverance of God's people.

Israel's small but elite group of fighter pilots is considered by many military experts to be the finest in the world. Zechariah 12 says that they will be strengthened by the Lord as they hold off the armies of the world in the War of Armageddon.

The Sea of Galilee can be seen at lower left in the photo.

Hal atop a Soviet-supplied Syrian tank that was captured by Israeli commandos in the Golan Heights.

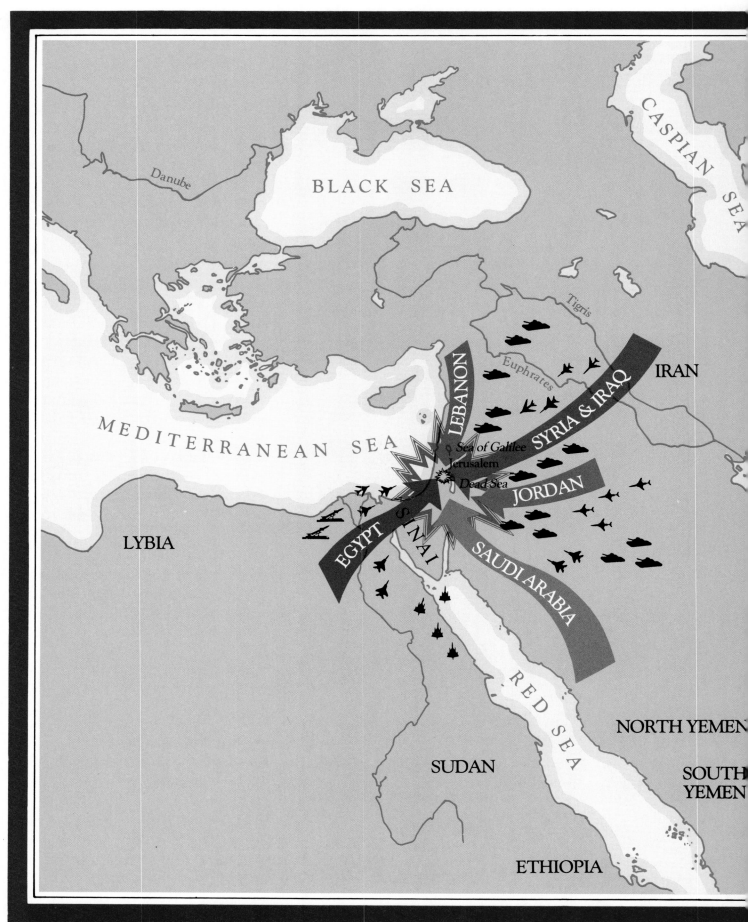

MAP 1 KING OF THE SOUTH

Pan-Arabic Armies Attack Israel. (*Daniel 11:40*)

First, Egyptian-led Pan-Arabic armies attack Israel. Long ago the psalmist predicted the final mad attempt of the confederated Arab armies to destroy the nation of Israel. Listen to what the Spirit of God predicted concerning this final attack that will begin the last war:

"O God, do not keep silent; be not quiet, O God, be not still. See how your enemies are astir, how your foes rear their heads. With cunning they conspire against your people; they plot against those you cherish. 'Come,' they say, 'Let us destroy them as a NATION, that the name of ISRAEL be remembered no more.'

"With one mind they plot together; they form an ALLIANCE against YOU—the tents of Edom and the Ishmaelites [Jordan], of Moab and the descendants of Hagar [most Arab people, including modern Egyptians], Gebal, Ammon and Amalek, Philistia [Palestinians], with the people of Tyre [Lebanon]. Even Assyria [Syria and Iraq] has joined them to lend strength to the descendants of Lot" (*Psalm 83:1-8 NIV*).

This prophecy sounds like Radio Damascus when it says, "Come, let us destroy them as a nation, that the name of Israel be remembered no more"!

The psalmist's prophecy quoted above indicates which armies will launch the initial attack. The prophet Daniel briefly describes this dreadful invasion: "At the time of the end [the middle of the Tribulation] the king of the South [the Egyptian-led Pan-Arabic armies] will engage him [Israeli False Prophet] in battle..." (*Daniel 11:40 NIV*).

The conditions in the Middle East are already setting the stage for this attack. The whole world is concerned about the volatile Arab-Israeli conflict that is always close to igniting a global war.

■ The Palestinians are determined to trouble the world until they repossess what they feel is their land.

■ The Arab nations consider it a matter of racial honor to destroy the State of Israel.

■ Islam considers it a sacred mission of religious honor to recapture Old Jerusalem and the El-Aqsa and Dome of the Rock mosques, which are located at the third-holiest site of their faith.

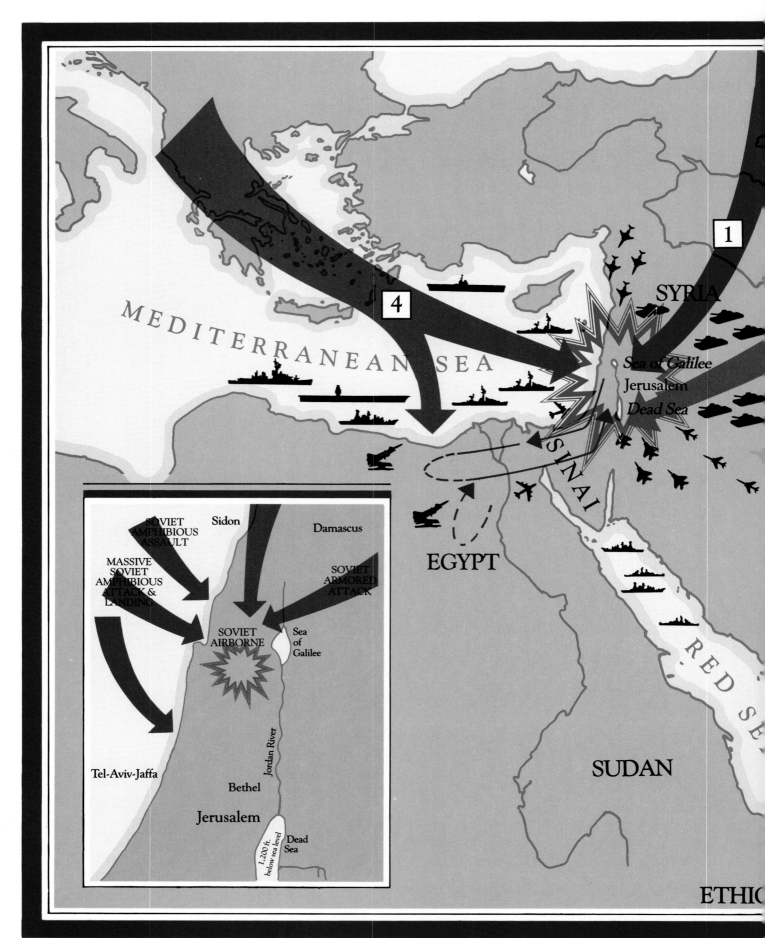

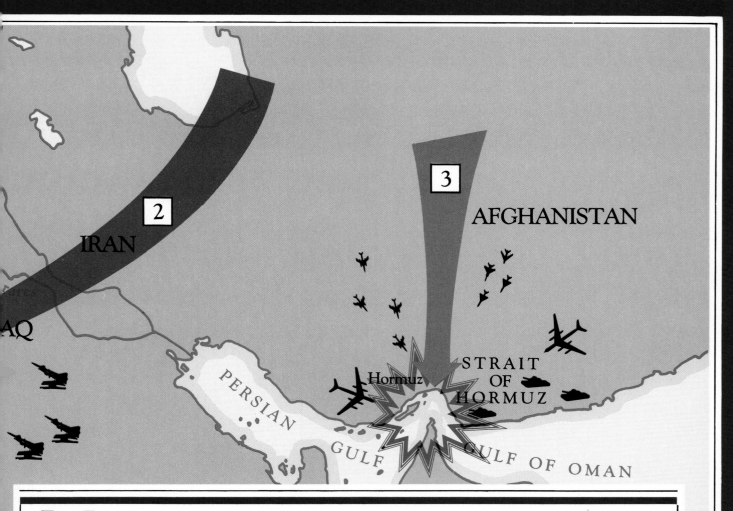

Map labels: IRAN, IRAQ (AQ), AFGHANISTAN, PERSIAN GULF, GULF OF OMAN, STRAIT OF HORMUZ, Hormuz

Map 2
KING OF THE NORTH

The Soviet Union Launches an All-Out Invasion.
(*Daniel 11:40-45*)

Phases:

1 & 2 Soviets and their allies launch massive invasion from land, sea, and air. Heavy use of tanks and armor.

3 Soviets launch lightning attack on Strait of Hormuz from Afghanistan to close off oil from Persian Gulf.

4 Soviet navy makes large amphibious invasion. Hits hard and lands at Haifa, gateway to the Valley of Armageddon. Also lands on shores of Egypt.

Soviet commander moves rapidly through Israel on his way to Egypt and prepares to take Africa. (*See Daniel 11:42-44.*)

News from north and east troubles the Soviet leader: The Red Chinese and ten-nation-led Western forces are mobilizing in preparation for counterattack. Soviet commander regroups and moves back to Jerusalem. Then he is destroyed by divine intervention.

Here at Haifa Bay the Soviets will make an amphibious invasion of Israel as part of the all-out War of Armageddon.

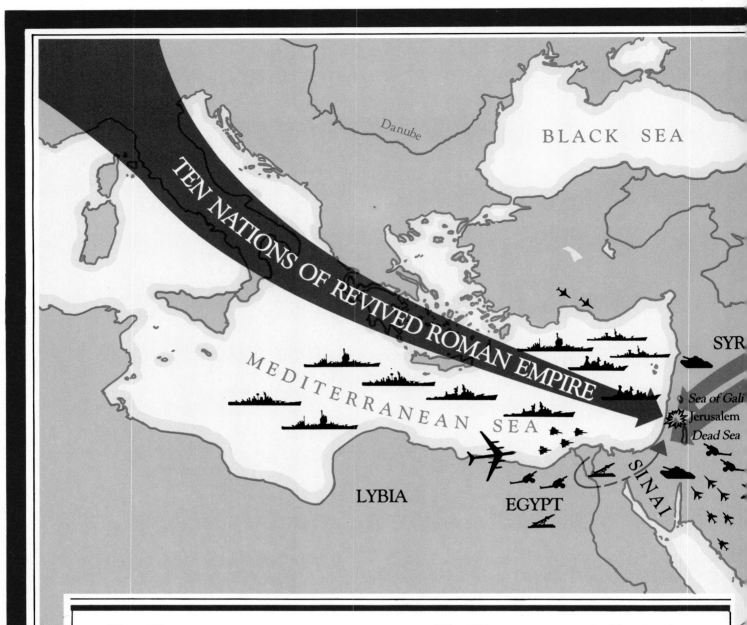

Danube

BLACK SEA

TEN NATIONS OF REVIVED ROMAN EMPIRE

MEDITERRANEAN SEA

SYR

Sea of Gali
Jerusalem
Dead Sea

SINAI

LYBIA

EGYPT

Map 3
ARMIES OF THE EAST AND WEST

Red China and Ten Nations of Europe Counterattack.
(*Revelation 16:12, Daniel 11:44*)

The Western nations led by the Antichrist and the oriental nations led by Red China attack the northern alliance of the Soviet Union. By both human and supernatural means, the Soviets are totally destroyed.

"I will drive the northern army [Soviets and their allies] far from you, pushing it into a parched and barren land, with its front columns going into the eastern sea and those in the rear into the western sea. And its stench

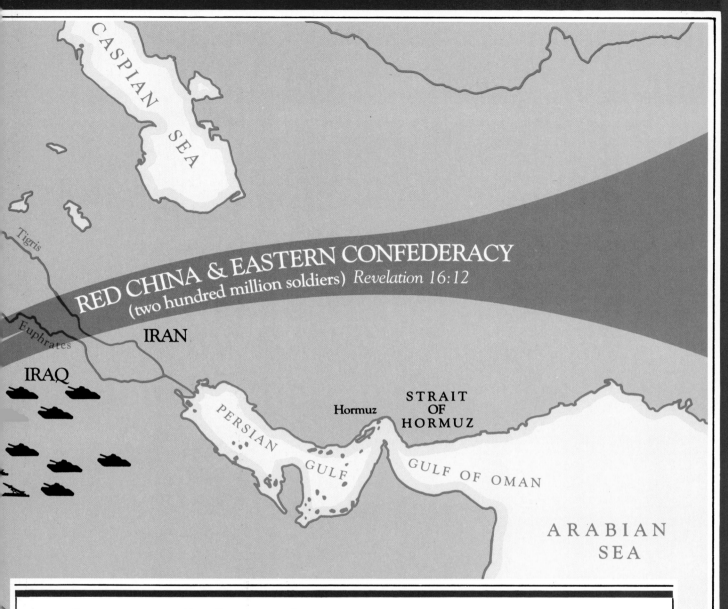

will go up; its smell will rise" (*Joel 2:20 NIV*).

"Son of man, prophesy against Gog [Soviet leader] and say: 'This is what the Sovereign Lord says: I am against you, O Gog, prince of Rosh, Meshech and Tubal. I will turn you around and drag you along. I will bring you from the far [extreme] north and send you against the mountains of Israel. Then I will strike your bow from your left hand and make your arrows drop from your right hand. On the mountains of Israel you will fall, you and all your troops and the nations with you. I will give you as food to all kinds of carrion birds and to the wild animals. You will fall in the open field, for I have spoken, declares the Sovereign Lord. I will send fire on Magog [the land of Russia] and on those who live in safety in the coastlands [the continents of the Gentile civilizations], and they will know that I am the Lord'" (*Ezekiel 39:1-6 NIV*).

The extensive Valley of Armageddon viewed from Mount Tabor, the traditional Mount of Transfiguration where the Messiah was revealed in His glory as the Son of God.

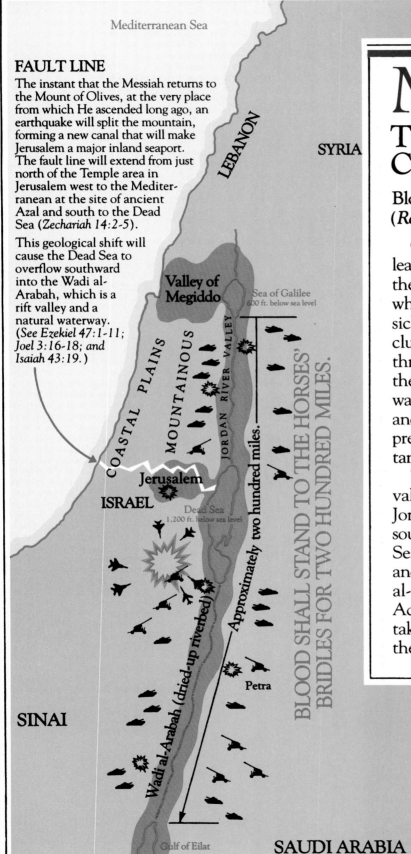

FAULT LINE

The instant that the Messiah returns to the Mount of Olives, at the very place from which He ascended long ago, an earthquake will split the mountain, forming a new canal that will make Jerusalem a major inland seaport. The fault line will extend from just north of the Temple area in Jerusalem west to the Mediterranean at the site of ancient Azal and south to the Dead Sea (*Zechariah 14:2-5*).

This geological shift will cause the Dead Sea to overflow southward into the Wadi al-Arabah, which is a rift valley and a natural waterway. (*See Ezekiel 47:1-11; Joel 3:16-18; and Isaiah 43:19.*)

Mediterranean Sea

LEBANON

SYRIA

Valley of Megiddo

Sea of Galilee
600 ft. below sea level

COASTAL PLAINS

MOUNTAINOUS

JORDAN RIVER VALLEY

Jerusalem

ISRAEL

Dead Sea
1,200 ft. below sea level

Approximately two hundred miles.

Wadi al-Arabah (dried-up riverbed)

Petra

SINAI

Gulf of Eilat

SAUDI ARABIA

BLOOD SHALL STAND TO THE HORSES' BRIDLES FOR TWO HUNDRED MILES.

Map 4
THE MESSIAH COMES

Blood Shall Stand to the Horses' Bridles. (*Revelation 14:19-20*)

One of the most-often-quoted and least-understood prophecies concerning the last days is Revelation 14:19-20, which says: "And the angel swung his sickle to the earth, and gathered the clusters from the vine of the earth, and threw them into the great wine press of the wrath of God. And the wine press was trodden outside the city [Jerusalem], and blood came out from the wine press, up to the horses' bridles, for a distance of two hundred miles."

The map shows the only continuous valley of that length in Israel. It is the Jordan River Valley, which extends southward from the southern end of the Sea of Galilee through the Dead Sea and dried-up river bed called the Wadi al-Arabah, to the Gulf of Eilat (or Aqabah). The fiercest fighting will take place around Jerusalem and along the Jordan Valley. Man will bring such horrible carnage upon himself that blood will stand to the horses' bridles along this Jordan Valley, most of which is below sea level.

Israel's Miraculous Deliverance

In one of the most incredible miracles of all time, Israel will be converted to faith in her true Messiah and then miraculously protected. The prophet Zechariah, whose name means "Jehovah remembers," promises an amazing deliverance: "In that day I will make the clans of Judah like a firepot among pieces of wood and a flaming torch among sheaves, so they will consume on the right hand and on the left all the surrounding peoples, while the inhabitants of Jerusalem again dwell on their own sites in Jerusalem. The Lord also will save the tents of Judah first in order that the glory of the house of David and the glory of the inhabitants of Jerusalem may not be magnified above Judah.

"In that day the Lord will defend the inhabitants of Jerusalem, and the one who is feeble among them in that day will be like David, and the house of David will be like God, like the angel of the Lord before them. And it will come about in that day that I will set about to destroy all the nations that come against Jerusalem" (*Zechariah 12:8-9*).

As promised, God will strengthen the Israelis to fight with a ferocity never seen before on this earth. He will also supernaturally protect them from being annihilated. The reason for all of this is given in the next verse: "And I will pour out on the house of David and on the inhabitants of Jerusalem, the Spirit of grace and of supplication, so that they will look on Me [the Messiah, the Lord Jesus] whom they [Israel] have pierced; and they will mourn for Him [the Messiah], as one mourns for an only son, and they will weep bitterly over Him, like the bitter weeping over a first-born" (*Zechariah 12:10*).

In this verse God Himself predicted that there would be a time when Israel would physically pierce Him. As we look through history, there is only one occasion on which this could have happened. It was when Israel nailed Jesus of Nazareth to the cross at Golgotha. This prophecy looks forward to that fateful moment when the sons of Israel will finally acknowledge that the One they pierced was none other than the God of Abraham, Jesus the Messiah.

SIGNS OF ARMAGEDDON'S APPROACH

All the conditions that the prophets have predicted would occur just before Armageddon are coming together before our eyes.

■ Israel has been reborn as a nation after centuries of dispersion.

■ Jerusalem is under Jewish sovereignty.

■ The exact foundation of the Jewish Temple has been discovered, triggering new ambitions of rebuilding it.

■ The Arab nations have united on the basis of their mutual desire to destroy the nation of Israel. Islam is pitted against Judaism.

■ The Soviet Union has arisen as the mightiest power in the world in fulfillment of Ezekiel, chapters 38 and 39.

■ Red China has become a formidable power with the manpower to fulfill the prophecies of Revelation 9 and 16:12.

■ Ten nations out of the ruins of the old Roman culture have united in the European Common Market. This is the beginning of the revived Roman Empire predicted in Daniel 7:23-28.

■ The general signs that Jesus predicted would precede His coming like "birth pains" are increasing in frequency and severity:

Religious deceptions.

International revolutions.

Wars and rumors of wars.

Earthquakes.

Famines caused by population explosion and weather changes.

Plagues.

Global weather changes with resulting killer storms.

Increasing lawlessness and crime.

All the predicted signs are before us. No other generation has ever witnessed the simultaneous coming together of these prophetic events. It is because of this that I believe we are the generation that will see the Lord Jesus' return.

A SURE HOPE

The Lord has promised that before the final seven years of worldwide catastrophe begin He will suddenly and secretly snatch up every living believer on earth. This event is commonly called the "Rapture" and is promised in passages like 1 Corinthians 15:51-53; 1 Thessalonians 4:15-18; 1 John 3:1-3; Philippians 3:20-21; Revelation 3:10; and 1 Thessalonians 1:10.

The Lord Jesus could come at any moment for His own who have believed in Him and have accepted the gift of forgiveness that He died in our place to provide. If you haven't received His pardon, invite Him to come into your life and forgive your sins and give you a new heart with new desires. Don't put it off...you may be playing Russian roulette with eternity.

I hope to see you on that great day, which is not far off.

The Kidron Valley winds between the walls of Old Jerusalem and the Mount of Olives. Part of the valley is a burial ground. Jeremiah (627-586 B.C.), who witnessed the destruction of Jerusalem and the Temple, prophesied that a day would come when *"The whole valley where dead bodies and ashes are thrown, and all the terraces out to the Kidron Valley on the east as far as the corner of the Horse Gate, will be holy to the Lord. The city will never again be uprooted or demolished"* (Jeremiah 31:40 NIV)

Information on tours to the Holy Land and cassette tapes by the author is available through Hal Lindsey Ministries:

Hal Lindsey Ministries
34 Malaga Cove Plaza
Palos Verdes Est., CA 90274

Hal and Kim Lindsey

PHOTOGRAPHERS

Dennis L. Pierce is an award-winning professional photographer located in Los Angeles, California. Recently he spent the better part of a year exploring major biblical sites in Israel, Egypt, Turkey, and Greece. Some of the photographic treasures he took appear in this book.

M. Nalbandian, owner of Garo Studio at Herod's Gate in Jerusalem, Israel, is one of the finest photographers in the Middle East.

Dick Lederhaus contributed some of the outstanding photographs he shot while serving as senior cinema photographer for World Wide Pictures. Mr. Lederhaus resides in Redondo Beach, California.

Philip Werman, president of Contract Supply Company in Fort Lauderhill, Florida, is a close personal friend of the author. An excellent amateur photographer, he was of great assistance during the author's photographic safari to Israel and preparation for this book.

Meron Ten-Brink is a licensed Israeli guide specializing in English-, Dutch-, German-, and Hebrew-speaking tours. The author's guide, he also contributed his photographic expertise to the photographic safari.

Larry Lundstrom, a frequent traveler to the Holy Land, contributed recent photographs from his extensive photographic library.

Note: All pictures not otherwise designated were taken by Hal and Kim Lindsey.

PHOTOGRAPH CREDITS

4 Kim Lindsey. 15-17 Meron Ten-Brink. 18 Dick Lederhaus. 19 Dennis Pierce. 20,21 Dennis Pierce. 22 World Wide Pictures. 23 Hal Lindsey. 24,25 Hal Lindsey. 26,27 Hal Lindsey. 28 Dennis Pierce. 29 Hal Lindsey. 30,31 Dennis Pierce. 32 Dennis Pierce. 34 Dennis Pierce. 35 NASA. 36 NASA. 38 Hal Lindsey. 39 Dennis Pierce. 40,41 Dennis Pierce. 42,43 Dick Lederhaus. 44 Hal Lindsey; *bottom*—Dennis Pierce. 45 Hal Lindsey. 46 Dick Lederhaus. 47 Dick Lederhaus. 49 Hal Lindsey. 50,51 Hal Lindsey. 52 Hal Lindsey. 53 Hal Lindsey. 54,55 Hal Lindsey. 56 *top*—Philip Werman; *bottom*—Dick Lederhaus. 57 Hal Lindsey. 58,59 Hal Lindsey. 60 Hal Lindsey. 61 Hal Lindsey. 62,63 Philip Werman. 64 Hal Lindsey. 65 *top left*—Dennis Pierce; *top right*—Dick Lederhaus; *bottom*— Hal Lindsey. 66 *top*—Kim Lindsey; *bottom left*—Hal Lindsey; *bottom right*—Hal Lindsey. 67 Hal Lindsey. 68,69 Hal Lindsey. 76,77 Larry Lundstrom. 78 *top*—Dick Lederhaus; *bottom*—Hal Lindsey. 79 M. Nalbandian. 80 Kim Lindsey. 81 Hal Lindsey. 82,83 M. Nalbandian. 84,85 M. Nalbandian. 86,87 Hal Lindsey. 89 Dick Lederhaus. 90 Dennis Pierce. 91 Hal Lindsey. 92 Dick Lederhaus. 93 Hal Lindsey. 94,95 Hal Lindsey. 96,97 Hal Lindsey. 98 Hal Lindsey. 100,101 Hal Lindsey. 102 Hal Lindsey. 103 Hal Lindsey. 105 Hal Lindsey. 106,107 Hal Lindsey. 109 Larry Lundstrom. 110,111 Dick Lederhaus. 112,113 Dick Lederhaus. 115 Dennis Pierce. 116,117 Hal Lindsey. 118 Dennis Pierce. 120,121 Hal Lindsey. 122,123 Hal Lindsey. 124 Hal Lindsey. 126,127 Hal Lindsey. 129 Hal Lindsey. 130,131 Hal Lindsey. 134,135 M. Nalbandian. 136,137 Don Mollenberg. 139 Kim Lindsey. 140,141 Dennis Pierce. 142,143 Hal Lindsey. 144,145 Hal Lindsey. 146,147 Hal Lindsey. 148 Hal Lindsey. 149 Hal Lindsey. 150,151 Hal Lindsey. 152,153 Hal Lindsey. 154,155 Kim Lindsey. 156,157 Hal Lindsey. 158,159 M. Nalbandian. 160,161 M. Nalbandian. 162,163 Larry Lundstrom. 164,165 M. Nalbandian. 166, 167 M. Nalbandian. 168 M. Nalbandian. 169 Hal Lindsey. 170,171 Dennis Pierce. 172 Hal Lindsey. 173 Dennis Pierce. 175 Kim Lindsey. 176,177 Hal Lindsey. 178,179 Dennis Pierce. 180,181 Dennis Pierce. 182,183 Dennis Pierce. 184,185 Hal Lindsey. 190,191 Hal Lindsey. 194,195 Hal Lindsey. 199 Hal Lindsey.